PRAISE FOR
Everything I Need *to* Know
I Learned *from* Other Women

"This book is a feast for the soul—there's something here for everyone. What a delicious collection of insights and inspiration for women!"

> —MARCI SHIMOFF, coauthor of *Chicken Soup for the Woman's Soul*

"This book provides an opportunity for both men and women to enjoy and learn about the feminine psyche and its deep capacity for building relationships, fostering communication, and deep nourishing of the human spirit."

> —ANGELES ARRIEN, Ph.D., cultural anthropologist, author of *The Fourfold Way* and *Signs of Life*

"As an actress, I am called upon to play a wide variety of roles. As a woman, I play even more—daughter, mother, friend, lover, artist, counselor, coach, nurse—the list seems endless! This book is a wonderful guide to playing all my roles more richly and fully."

> —KELLY LYNCH, actress

"I hear the voices of many women in this wonderful book—voices of inspiration, voices of courage, voices of common sense. Wise women from different backgrounds share important lessons about life, love, family, money, success, disappointment, and the meaning of it all. I am enriched by reading this inspiring collection of women's wisdom."

> —MARCIA SELIGSON, Producing Artistic Director, REPRISE! Broadway's Best

"BJ Gallagher's well of wisdom and encouragement seems bottomless. She gives life to the maxim that sisterhood is powerful."

> —SUSAN PAGE, author of *If We're So In Love, Why Aren't We Happy?*

"This wonderful book is filled with wise, witty, useful stories and tidbits about life I wish I had learned when I was fifteen!"

> —ARIELLE FORD, author of *Hot Chocolate for the Mystical Soul*

Everything I Need *to* Know
I Learned *from* Other
Women

Everything I Need *to* Know
I Learned *from* Other
Women

BJ Gallagher

CONARI PRESS

We gratefully acknowledge permission to reprint the following: Excerpted from *Do As I Say, Not As I Did* by Wendy Reid Crisp. Copyright © 1997 by Wendy Reid Crisp. Reprinted by permission of Berkeley Publishing Group.

Cover Photography: © Hulton Archive/Getty Images, Inc.
Cover Handtinted by Peggy Lindt, Point Blank Design
Cover and book design: Suzanne Albertson

Library of Congress Cataloging-in-Publication Data
Hateley, B. J. Gallagher (Barbara J. Gallagher), 1949-
Everything I need to know I learned from other women / BJ Gallagher.
     p.   cm.
ISBN 1-57324-859-2
1. Women—Psychology. 2. Women—Conduct of life. I. Title.
    HQ1206 .H345 2002   2002009408
    305.4—dc21

Printed in Canada.

04 05 TC 10 9 8 7 6

To my mother, Gloria Gallagher,

the most important woman in my life

Everything I Need *to* Know
I Learned *from* Other Women

By Way of *Introduction* . . .

WHEN I WAS A LITTLE GIRL, I thought that when kids became grownups, they stopped changing – that adulthood was a state of stability. Once you grew up, I figured, that was it – you were you. But when I became an adult, I learned that I had been mistaken – the growing never stops. And the learning never stops . . . if I am open to it. Over the years I have learned from books and newspapers, from movies and TV, from preachers and teachers, as well as from my own life experiences – but mostly I have learned from other women.

My mother was the first woman in my life, and she is still the most important. But she was not my only teacher. Other women have also been powerful influences on me – on my thinking, on my ability to relate to men, on my career, and on the kind of person I am today. Among these are friends, relatives, friends of friends, professors, authors, spiritual women, secular women, artists, neighbors, professional colleagues, and many, many more. I've been influenced by women I didn't know personally: women authors, poets, and musicians, women in the movies and on TV, political women, women in religion, famous women, notorious women – many of them have taught me important lessons. Each woman has left a bit of herself with me – an indelible imprint on my psyche, on my soul.

Women learning from other women is the theme of this book. In compiling stories for this book, I wanted to include not only lessons from women in my own life, but from others' lives as well. I asked friends and family; I inquired among my professional colleagues; I sent out Internet queries; and I even pestered friends while we were vacationing together in Mexico. I asked lots of questions:

Where is it that you learned the important lessons of life?

Who are your teachers, your role models?

Where do you look to understand what it means to be a woman, how to live a fulfilled life, how to decide what's important, and what's the meaning of it all?

I hope the stories I have gathered in this book might help you live your life a bit happier, a tad healthier, and maybe with a smidgen more fun, too! True wisdom is the ability to learn from other people's experiences – without having to go out and reinvent the wheel. This book is my gift to you – may it bring you a little bit of wisdom and lots of inspiration.

With love and laughter,

BJ Gallagher

I

Attitude Is Everything

Nobody can be exactly like me.
Sometimes even I have
trouble doing it.

—*Tallulah Bankhead, actress*

- "Happiness is available...help yourself" reads the sign on the wall over Anita's desk.
- "Mind over matter," my mother reminds me.
- *Happiness Is a Choice* is the book on my friend Jackie's coffee table.
- "You'll see it when you believe it — not vice versa!" the seminar leader asserts.
- "BJ, you need an attitude adjustment today," my friend Anne scolds me.

I am grateful for the regular reminders of how important attitude is because sometimes I forget. I need these messages every so often — like little Post-it™ notes from the Universe — so I'll remember how my attitude affects my relationships with other people, how it influences the quality of my work, how it impacts my health, and how it determines how much I enjoy life.

Other women have taught me much about the critical role that attitude plays — in good times and in bad. Most importantly, they taught me that I can *choose* my own attitude! It's not something immutable in my DNA over which I have no control. My attitude is not cast in concrete — in any given moment I can choose to change it. I may not be able to control what happens in the world around me, but I can certainly control how I respond to it.

It's true what they say, "What you expect is what you get." Attitude is everything.

It's Mind over Matter

MY MOTHER WAS TERRIFIC at turning negatives into positives. We were a military family, which meant that every few years, sometimes every few months, we had to pick up and move to a new city or town – sometimes a new country! I always lamented the loss of my friends whenever we had to move. And my mother invariably said, "You're not losing your friends; you get to keep them, and you get to make some new ones too!" She wasn't just rationalizing – she genuinely believed it. She had this instinctive ability to take problems and turn them into opportunities, to find the proverbial silver lining in whatever clouds came her way.

Psychologists have a fancy term for this – they call it reframing the situation. How you respond to something emotionally is a function of how you frame it cognitively. If you think about moving as a loss, then you will feel grief and sadness. If you think about moving as a new adventure, then you will feel excitement and anticipation. My mother didn't have a degree in psychology, but she instinctively understood how to reframe situations for herself and her children. This ability is one of the most valuable legacies I inherited from my mother.

Mom knew that children often take their cues from their parents. If parents are upset by a situation, their kids will be too. If parents take things in stride and adapt to change quickly and easily, chances are, so will the kids. She understood the importance of modeling the kind of behavior you want from your children. She viewed each move in a positive manner, looking forward to the opportunity to move into a new house or apartment and decorate it, enjoying the creative challenge posed by changing "nests" frequently. (Dad often joked that whenever Mom got our home fixed up just the way she liked it, she'd look at Dad and say, "I'm done now. I guess it's time to move again!" And often it was.)

Mom enjoyed the packing and sorting, the organizing and weeding out. She liked finding new things in the new location to create a warm, homey environment for us. We didn't have a lot of money, but she was resourceful in buying things from thrift shops, making things herself, and finding bargains in antique stores. She made moving an adventure for herself, and she taught me to do the same.

There were other ways in which her philosophy about attitude influenced my own ideas about attitude. One of her favorite sayings was, "Mind over matter." She invoked this mantra whenever I was whining or complaining (as kids often do). "Mind over matter" was an all-purpose panacea for assorted and sundry problems. Feeling lonely? Instead of focusing on your aloneness as a problem, view it as an opportunity to do something that requires solitude, like writing or cleaning your closet. Unhappy because of bad weather? Look at it as an opportunity to stay indoors and get something done. Feeling sad because something or someone disappointed you? Make a gratitude list and see all the wonderful things you have going for you!

Over the years, I had many opportunities to see how Mom's "mind over matter" mantra worked in all sorts of life situations.

I even went so far as to see if it would work with jet lag! I travel a lot on business, and like most people, I used to feel tired and a bit disoriented whenever my destination was in a different time zone. I just accepted it as jet lag.

About ten years ago, while on a business trip to Denmark, I decided to try an experiment with jet lag — to see if "mind over matter" would work on it. The plane left Los Angeles. When it was light outside, I stayed awake. When we flew over the North Pole and it was dark, I slept. When we arrived in Copenhagen, I set my watch on local time, two o'clock in the afternoon, and proceeded with the rest of my day, seeing some of the sights and having dinner with a friend. I never allowed myself to think about what time it was in Los Angeles. As far as I was concerned, the local time was the only time that was relevant. I went to sleep that night at my usual time, and got up the next morning at my usual time. I experienced no jet lag. Son of a gun, "mind over matter" really worked!

What's more, I've never had jet lag since then. I fly coast to coast with no problem. Time zones don't phase me a bit. I just set my watch on the local time, and that's what time it is for me. I don't think about what time it is back home. It's not important. What is important is that I don't get jet lag.

My mother taught me volumes about the power of the human mind and my ability to choose my attitude in any situation. Reframing problems into opportunities and practicing "mind over matter" — these attitudinal lessons have made my life easier and more fun. Thanks, Mom.

Dear BJ,

It's so hard, even at my age, to admit that my mother has valuable words of wisdom:

"Nothing changes but the attitude, and everything changes."

I was reminded of it by a recent "Zits" cartoon where the kid, Jeremy, is very grouchy over breakfast. His mother is obnoxiously cheerful and suggests many reasons to be happy – beautiful day, etc. The last frame shows Jeremy leaving the house, grumbling that he hates to admit it, but his mother is right. She's just ruined a perfectly good funk.

Well, I hate to admit it, but my mother is right. You can change the way you look at things, and it does make a difference. It's all in the category of taking responsibility for your own life.

Regards,
Lynn Shaffer, architect

What do you hang on the walls of your mind?

—**Eve Arnold**, photographer

*Life is raw material. We are artisans. We can
sculpt our existence into something beautiful,
or debase it into ugliness. It's in our hands.*

—**Cathy Better**, poet, writer, editor

Cultivating an Attitude of Gratitude

The mind is a mismatch detector. It always notices what's wrong before it notices what's right. This isn't all bad — it's the way our brains are hardwired to ensure our safety and survival. Millions of years ago, if you came home to your cave and your few possessions were not as you had left them, you were instantly alerted to the threat of an intruder. Same thing today — when you notice something out of place, a warning signal goes off in your brain, sending you the message: "Something's wrong here . . . be alert!" It serves you well to have your brain scanning for what's wrong.

The problem is, too much of a good thing becomes a liability. Many of us have cultivated fault finding to a high art — noticing every little thing that could be better in each and every situation.

continued

We drive people around us crazy with it, and we induce a state of chronic dissatisfaction in ourselves.

My friend Kym taught me to make gratitude lists, to balance out the fault finding that naturally takes place in my mind. It is a way of retraining my brain and refocusing my attention on what's right, rather than what's wrong. Doing a gratitude list will pull me out of my critical mode almost instantly. It is also a good antidote to self-pity and depression.

Here are just some of the many things I'm grateful for:

- My good health
- Intelligence and creativity
- My growing, changing spiritual life
- Lovely weather where I live
- My sweet little hilltop house
- My wonderful cats
- Healthy family members
- My reliable car
- The many freedoms I enjoy as an American
- Friends who love me
- Making my living writing and teaching
- Laughter and surprises
- Mandy Patinkin concerts and Anthony Hopkins movies

and so much more. . .

What are the things on your gratitude list?

The Buddha walked away from his wife while she was sleeping. I don't want to go anywhere, I don't want to leave anybody behind. Happiness is right here, right now, in this world, in this room. I am happiest wherever it is that I am.

—Alexandra Stoddard, author of
Choosing Happiness

What Will You Do with Two More Years?

In 1996, the life expectancy for women stood at seventy-nine years; for men, it was seventy-three years. Projections for 2010 show life expectancy will be eighty-one years and seventy-four years, respectively.

A Wonderful Hat
Makes all the Difference!

I HAVE MY OWN PERSONAL "Auntie Mame." Eccentric, colorful, entertaining, exasperating, larger than life, and impossibly outrageous, she is Eloise Elizabeth Jensen Chamberlain Kozak. She is my mother's sister — and you couldn't find two more different women. My mother is bookish, shy, and introverted, preferring her garden and her cats to people. Auntie El, as I call her, is extraverted, extravagant, talkative, and always the center of attention. Both women were stylish when they were younger — but it was Eloise who really had the flair for putting herself together. She bought expensive designer clothes and took superb care of them, making them last for years.

As she got older, Auntie El put on weight, a lot of it. But she still managed to look handsome and elegant somehow. I marveled at how she could do that. Whenever I gain weight, I just want to cover it all up with XL T-shirts and straight-leg jeans. But Auntie El would never be caught dead in jeans. She wore pearls, a heavy gold bracelet, her emerald and diamond rings, beautiful expensive shoes, and flowing colorful caftans. She looked like an aging film star — zaftig and boozy, but still a commanding presence.

And then there were the hats — she always loved hats. She wore classy, sophisticated hats in the '40s and '50s, when she lived in San Francisco. When she and Uncle Andrew moved to Sedona, Arizona, about sixteen years ago, she started wearing Western-style broad-brimmed hats — each with its own stunning hatband. My favorite was a brown suede Stetson, trimmed with a narrow black leather band studded with genuine turquoise nuggets. When she walked into a room with that hat, everyone took notice.

I went to visit Auntie El in Sedona a couple of years ago, and over lunch one afternoon I commented on her beautiful collection of hats. She smiled knowingly and leaned over to whisper something so that her husband wouldn't overhear: "I wear these stunning hats so that people will look at my face and not my big tush!" she confided conspiratorially. She was right — that's exactly what people did.

Auntie El summarized succinctly what generations of women have been doing for hundreds — no, thousands — of years. She understands the power that clothing and accessories have to draw the eye to the most appealing part of the female body. Auntie El's couture lesson was not news to me, but it distilled the essence of female fashion wisdom in such a simple sentence that it stuck with me. Today, whenever I try on hats, I think of Auntie El.

A good hat can make the difference between a bimbo and a princess.

  —Robin Williams' mom (Robin played Mrs. Doubtfire
    in the movie of the same name)

Chicago Sun Times: "People today are wearing things on their T-shirts that they once wouldn't dare tell their analysts."

WOMEN'S T-SHIRTS WITH ATTITUDE

- Veni, Vedi, Visa (I Came. I Saw. I Did a Little Shopping.)
- Coffee, Chocolate, Men ... Some things are just better rich.
- Old age comes at a bad time.
- Princess, having had sufficient experience with princes, seeks frog.
- My mother is a travel agent for guilt trips.
- If they don't have chocolate in heaven, I ain't going.
- So many men, so few who can afford me.
- Do NOT start with me. You will NOT win.
- Warning: I have an attitude and I know how to use it.

If you obey all the rules
you miss all the fun.

—Katherine Hepburn, actress

If you can't be a good example,
then you'll just have to be a horrible warning.

—Catherine Aird, author of witty British police novels

From birth to 18 a girl needs good parents;
from 18 to 35 she needs good looks;
from 35 to 55 she needs a good personality;
and from 55 on she needs cash.

—Sophie Tucker, vaudeville entertainer

Catching More Flies with Honey

IT'S FUNNY THE THINGS in our lives that leave such a lasting impression. Sometimes something very simple can have life-changing impact. When I was in junior high school I had a sub-scription to *Seventeen* magazine, which I eagerly devoured each month as soon as it arrived. I was the daughter of a military family, and we were stationed overseas during those years. Being an American teenager in a foreign country, I sensed I was missing out on important experiences of being a teen in America, and I was hungry to fill this void in any way I could, including reading *Seventeen.*

The message of one particular article imprinted itself permanently in my impressionable teenaged brain. I don't know the name of the woman who wrote the story, but this unknown writer is responsible for a critical turning point in my life.

The article was about how to attract boys. Its message was clear and simple: Boys like to spend time with girls who are cheerful, upbeat, friendly, and warm. They do not like to be with girls who are depressed, surly, cranky, and cold. It may not seem like such a big deal today, but at the time, that article's message was seared into my consciousness. It caused me to make a decision — one of those Life Decisions: I decided to be cheerful and upbeat in all circumstances. I was very interested in attracting boys, and if this is what would do it, then so be it!

Of course, my mother would probably say that she could have

told me this without my having to read it in a magazine. In fact, she did tell me this in other words at different times in my life. Her words were, "You catch more flies with honey than with vinegar." She wasn't talking about attracting boys – she was talking about dealing with other people in general. I came to agree with my mother and generalized what I call "the power of cheerfulness" into many other life situations. It helped me in school, in social settings, and in job situations, anytime I was interacting with other people.

For instance, when I was in my twenties and working as a waitress, I used to view grumpy customers as a personal challenge, to see if I could turn them around during the course of a meal. The more unpleasant they were, the more I poured "emotional honey" over them. It was a game that I played with them, unbeknownst to them, of course! And guess what? It worked more times than not. Not only did I feel the satisfaction of having met a personal challenge, I often got a good tip, to boot!

It's funny how often I have read articles or books that have taught me something important and useful and then shared that information with my mother – only to have her reply, "I've been telling you that for years!" I don't know why is it that kids (adult kids, too) will readily heed the advice of experts but ignore the very same advice when it's uttered by their parents. All I know is that the *Seventeen* magazine writer who wrote that story made a lightbulb go on in my head. Whoever she was, thank you.

Mirror, Mirror, on the Wall . . .
Which of These Women Has It All?

Approachable	**OR**	Angry
Teachable		Testy
Tireless		Tiresome
Inspired		Irritable
Terrifically optimistic		Terribly pessimistic
Upbeat		Upset
Determined		Depressed
Eager to find solutions		Eager to assign blame

Sometimes Even
Eagles Need a Push

MANY OF US HAVE BEEN INFLUENCED and inspired by famous and accomplished women as we read about them in newspapers and magazines. Some of us are even fortunate enough to have been influenced by a famous woman in a much more personal way. My friend Chris Phillips had one of those "close encounters of the most important kind" with a woman who subsequently went on to become First Lady, the wife of our forty-first president.

Chris's life-changing conversation occurred about fifteen years ago, when she and her husband attended a literacy conference in their hometown in Michigan. Barbara Bush, who has been active in promoting literacy for many decades, was the keynote speaker. At the time, George Bush was vice president, campaigning to become president.

After the conference, select people were invited to a local judge's house for tea with Mrs. Bush. Chris and her husband were invited to attend, since they were both active in their community. It was a lovely afternoon with lots of stimulating conversation about local issues, national politics, and, of course, literacy.

At one point during the afternoon, Chris excused herself to go find the ladies' room. Discovering a line of women waiting to use the facilities, she took her place in line. The next thing she knew, Barbara Bush got in line behind her, and the two struck up a conversation about jobs and families. They began a mother-to-mother talk about children's education. The conversation turned from their children to themselves, and Mrs. Bush encouraged Chris to take more of a leadership position in her community – to stretch beyond her self-imposed boundaries.

Chris replied, "Oh, I couldn't do that. I don't have the education." At the time, she had an AA degree from the local community college and was a secretary at the Michigan headquarters of an international company.

"What's holding you back?" Mrs. Bush asked. "What are the barriers in your way to going on to get a bachelors degree? Are they external barriers – lack of money, child care responsibilities, an unsupportive husband? Or are they internal barriers – lack of self-confidence, doubt, insecurity? You have to identify the barriers to see what's holding you back."

"Well...," Chris replied, mulling over Mrs. Bush's question, "I guess they're mostly internal barriers. I'm just a secretary; I guess I never thought about taking on more."

"Well!" Mrs. Bush harrumphed in her best maternal manner, "you have to take the initiative to develop yourself! No one is going to do it for you. No one is holding you back – you're holding yourself back. Stay in touch with other women – let them encourage you and help you. Get that education! You can become a leader!"

The two women were standing just inches apart. Barbara Bush's face and words left an indelible impression in Chris's mind. The seeds had been planted...

Chris submitted her application to the Community Leadership

Academy, an organization devoted to the development of up-and-coming community leaders. She was accepted, becoming the first secretary from her company ever to attend.

When Chris successfully completed the Academy, she thought to herself, "If I can do that who knows what else I can do?" She decided to go back to college and get her bachelors degree. She enrolled in Spring Arbor College and completed the sixty units she needed to finish her degree in just fifty-five weeks!

Upon graduation, Chris wrote to Barbara Bush (who was now First Lady), telling her of her accomplishments and thanking her for being the catalyst in Chris' pursuit of higher education and leadership development. Mrs. Bush replied, congratulating Chris and encouraging her to continue as far as her drive and ambition would carry her.

Chris was unstoppable now. She submitted an application for a $10,000 grant to the W. K. Kellogg Foundation to develop an "expert in residence" program for Calhoun County. Working with the AIDS Coordinating Council, she used her grant money to bring Jeannie White, the mother of AIDS patient Ryan White, to her community to conduct HIV/STD and AIDS awareness training programs for participants from the city, county, and state.

Chris moved on to pursue a masters degree, which she completed in three years. At last report, Chris was getting ready to apply for a Ph.D. program. She still works full-time as a diversity associate business partner and program leader specializing in programs for women and people of color. In addition, she is an adjunct professor at the local community college, teaching non-traditional evening college students. She has also raised two terrific kids and has celebrated twenty-five years of marriage with her supportive, wonderful husband.

Barbara Bush probably had no idea the impact her words, spoken years ago at an afternoon political tea, would have. Chris had the talent, skill, and energy to go far in life – but needed a kick in the butt to get going. Barbara Bush gave her that loving but firm kick. Chris was smart as well as lucky – she accepted the attitude adjustment that Barbara Bush offered her. She used it to leap from the safety of her self-imposed comfy little nest and try her wings in the big, wide world. She was like a young eagle who just needed a little push to get her started – someone who believed in her when she did not believe in herself.

We should all be so lucky to have someone – famous or not – give us that nudge, that push, that kick in the butt to get us started. We are often our own worst enemies, subverting our future with self-doubt and self-limiting beliefs. Where can you turn for that push, that loving kick in the butt, when you need it?

What separates an ordinary woman from an extraordinary one?
The belief that she is ordinary.

—Jody Williams, 1997 Nobel Peace Prize winner

I believe talent is like electricity. We do not understand electricity. We use it. Electricity makes no judgement. You can plug into it, and light up a lamp, keep a heart pump going, light a cathedral, or you can electrocute a person with it. . . . I think talent is like that. I believe every person is born with a talent.

—Maya Angelou, poet, professor, actress, author

What Are You Afraid of?
Turn Your *Fear* into a *Possibility*...

FEAR	POSSIBILITY
Making decisions?	Owning your own life.
Making mistakes?	Learning valuable lessons.
Failing?	Starting over.
Being alone?	Enjoying your own company.
Losing your love?	Finding new loves.
Losing your job?	Beginning a new challenge.
Having no money?	Living more simply and resourcefully.
Getting older?	Accepting change gracefully.
Death?	Understanding life.
Not getting what you want?	Wanting what you have.

To name your fears is to dissolve them.

Freedom Is the
Mother of Reinvention

SAY WHAT YOU LIKE ABOUT Madonna's music or her choice of men, you have to give her credit for the way she has reinvented herself over the years. Christopher Lasch once wrote a book called *Protean Man,* about how people in modern America have the freedom and ability to transform themselves, taking on different personas and different identities over time. I think Madonna is the quintessential Protean Woman.

She started off more than twenty years ago as a slightly chubby sex kitten, wearing her bad girl clothes and her crucifix. Then she morphed into the hard-body macho girl, playing "Truth or Dare" with fans and critics alike. She went through a highly sexualized phase, writing her hugely successful book, *SEX.* She moved on to become a literal madonna, a mother with child – not once, but twice. Deciding to explore her spirituality in depth, she became involved with yoga and Kabbalah and brought her personal spirituality into her music. Finally, she decided to get married in a Scottish castle and move to the U.K. She's a veritable human chameleon – changing hairstyles, fashions, musical genres, and identities faster than a lizard can change his colors.

The Protean Woman reminds me that I, too, have the power to recreate myself over and over again, as many times as I want. I can try on new identities much like I might try on a new coat or experiment with a new hairstyle. The freedom I have as a woman living in the Western Hemisphere at this point in history means I can be a tomboy, a scholar, a vamp, a priest, a cynic, a party girl, a homebody, a hermit, or whatever else strikes my fancy. As long as I can support myself, and don't hurt anyone else or infringe on their rights, I too can be a Protean Woman. I might get some flak for my choices, but my life is my own. My only limit is my creativity, imagination, and energy.

Now ... where's that pointy, cone-shaped bra I wanted to wear tonight?

You don't have to decide what you're going to be, ever.
You can be something different every day if you want.

—Laurie Anderson's mom (Laurie is a musician ...
at least for today)

If we do not rise to the challenge of our unique capacity to shape our lives, to seek the kinds of growth that we find individually fulfilling, then we can have no security. We will live in a world of sham, in which our selves are determined by the will of others, in which we will be constantly buffeted and increasingly isolated by the changes around us.

—Nena O'Neil, author

Dear BJ,

When I lived in Laguna Beach we had a neighbor who was about as exotic as you could be – a raving beauty, full of life and sex appeal (I wouldn't have called it that then, I was only thirteen or so). She lived alone; her little boy, whom she visited regularly, lived with his father in Mexico. She was always having spectacular parties with sophisticated people, live music, and would dress in black leotards, ballet slippers, and big silver hoop earrings. She designed clothing and had a great following, mostly Hollywood types.

One day, she asked me if I'd like to model for her at a trunk show in Beverly Hills... I thought I'd died and gone to heaven! I modeled "younger girl" versions of her creations; it was a big thrill, but what I came away with was a knowledge that you can do anything you want if you are willing to put into it what it takes. I will never forget how independent, daring, and waaaaay out of the box she was. And probably still IS! I didn't end up being a model, but she planted an image in my imagination – an image of freedom and flamboyance – that influences me to this day.

Cheers,
Robin Lehman

You were once wild here. Don't let them tame you.

—Isadora Duncan, founder of modern dance

What Is a WOMAN?

Wise

Original

Miraculous

Aware

Natural

2

Friends Forever

Friends are the family you
choose for yourself.

—*Sandra Magsamen, artist*

Where would I be if it weren't for my women friends? We laugh together, cry together, compare notes on our children, and complain about our jobs. We do lunch, we go shopping, we borrow each other's clothes, and we talk on the phone ... for hours sometimes. I depend on them for so much — company, comfort, guidance, advice, and sometimes a good swift kick when I need it!

I can't begin to list all the things I have learned from women about friendship — starting from when I was a little girl. In our girlish play, we practiced life skills — playing house, playing school, and playing dress-up. We learned how to deal with conflicts and hurt feelings; we learned about competition and cooperation; we learned about celebration as well as disappointment.

Whether we are black or white, fat or thin, outgoing or shy, rich or poor, old or young, we are first and foremost female. Our common bond of feminine experience is stronger than any differences. There is something so essential and primordial in women sharing with other women. It seems the most natural thing in the world. Give me the support of a few good women friends, and I can do almost anything!

Ebony and Ivory

IT WAS THE END OF THE YEAR. Ruth Pawluk and I were savoring that wonderful eggnog latte that Starbucks serves only during December. We were both in a reflective mood, thinking about the people who were most important in our lives.

"I have this wonderful friend, Brunetta," Ruth said as she blew softly at the foam on her latte. "She and I are an unlikely pair of friends, at least on the surface. Brunetta is ninety-two and I'm thirty-nine; she is black and I am white; she has been married three times and I haven't had even one husband yet!"

I laughed at the plaintive tinge in her voice when she got to the husband part. Ruth laughed too.

"I met Brunetta about ten years ago and we have been fast friends ever since," Ruth continued. "On the surface we seem very different, but underneath we are really kindred spirits. We are both educated, well traveled, worldly, and in the theater. Brunetta's third husband was a well-respected off-Broadway producer, and she's regaled me with stories of her show-business life – barbecues with Arthur Miller and Marilyn Monroe, being escorted to an opening night by Sean Connery, being seated next to Jean Renoir, and glamorous things like that. Brunetta's husband died just as he was hitting the big time, and James Earl Jones gave the eulogy at his funeral.

"She has had an amazing, exciting life – living for a time in Europe, developing a passion for bullfighting, indulging in a dangerous love affair, working with Langston Hughes and Lorraine Hansbury in Chicago, and so much more. The thing that has most impressed me about Brunetta is her story about how her life really began at fifty-two. She left her husband in the Midwest and moved to New York just because she loved the theater – can you imagine that? This renegade black woman leaving her marriage and her security to traipse off to New York and start a new life in her fifties! She calls that the beginning of her halcyon years – and that has always given me hope."

"Hope?" I asked Ruth. "Hope for what?"

"Hope that my life can still be wonderful. I feel like I've been so slow to blossom – not married yet, no kids, no house, I drive an old car, and I'm nowhere near the level of achievement I would have expected by now. I feel like I'm just beginning to take my acting and theater work seriously – and here I am, thirty-nine already!

"But Brunetta has taught me that life is ongoing – that even in the middle of life, one can pick up and create something totally new. If Brunetta's halcyon years began at fifty-two, then there's hope for me! I can change course anytime I want – at fifty-two, sixty-two, seventy-two – or even thirty-nine."

"Sounds like she's a really important friend," I replied.

"She is. And I miss her. She lives back in Chicago now, with her sister Lillian, who cares for her in the loving manner she deserves," Ruth said. "I call her when I need to talk about what's happening in the world, in my life, and when I just need to talk to someone older and wiser than I. Sometimes I call just to check in and see how my soul sister is doing. Having Brunetta in my life reminds me not to look back with regret at time wasted, but rather look forward to what's still to come."

A friend is someone you can be alone with and have nothing to do and not be able to think of anything to say and be comfortable in the silence.

—Sheryl Condie, poet

Friends Are Beautiful People

Over the years, I've learned that holidays wouldn't be holidays without good friends. Sometimes family hassles make the holidays difficult and painful — but friends can create a family-of-choice with whom to spend our holidays. In the past twenty years, I've spent more than a few happy Christmas mornings at the home of my friends Eva Schindler Rainman and Barbara Powers. Tradition-ally they have an open house, inviting friends to drop by and enjoy a nosh along with a "Beautiful People Drink." The fire crackles in the fireplace, the house smells of fresh pine and baked goods, and warm, friendly faces smile and talk, accompanied by the clink-clink of wine glasses toasting one another. We catch up with friends we haven't seen since the previous year; we meet new people who haven't been there before; and we munch and sip our way through the morning. It's hard to have a bad Christmas if you start it off with friends and beautiful people.

continued

Eva and Barbara moved away about eight years ago, and Eva died unexpectedly just a month later. Today, my head still turns automatically when I drive by their old house, as if I expect to see my friends' silhouettes through the living room picture window.

When Christmas comes around, I sometimes make a batch of "Beautiful People Drinks" and invite a few friends over. I'm sure Eva is smiling, wherever she is.

Beautiful People Drinks

Ingredients

Chilled champagne

Southern Comfort

Canned apricot halves

Directions

Open the can of apricot halves.

Spoon one apricot half into each space in the ice cube tray; pour a little of the juice over each apricot, filling up the space.

Freeze apricots overnight.

When you're ready to serve, remove ice cube tray from freezer.

Pop the apricot ice cubes out of the tray; and place one in each stemmed glass (champagne glasses are a little small; better to use bigger wine glasses).

Pour a shot of Southern Comfort into each glass; then fill to the top with champagne.

Serve and enjoy!

If any of the people at your party are not beautiful, they *will* be, once you have a couple of these!

Listening Is the Greatest Gift

IN MY EARLY TWENTIES, I was hired to be an interviewer for a research project being conducted by some professors at the University of Delaware — it was a statewide study on housing for the elderly. My job was to drive around the state and interview old people about their housing. Some of them lived in retirement complexes, some lived in their own homes, some lived with relatives, and a few lived in really unusual places — like the old man who lived in a chicken coop. A woman named Suzanne trained several of us students to be good interviewers. I remember her well, because she taught me one of the most important things I have ever learned.

The training included all the elements of good interviewing training: what to tell participants about the research, how to get their permission, how to fill out the interview protocol, how to keep track of time, and how to bring closure to the end of the interview. In addition, we were taught to keep track of our mileage, submit our work on a weekly basis, and participate in analyzing the data, particularly the open-ended questions.

Throughout the training, I had a nagging doubt that kept tugging at the edge of my consciousness. Finally, on the last day of training, I asked Suzanne, "Why will these old people want to talk to us? These questionnaires we have to fill out are pretty long and boring — I doubt that they'll give us the time of day. Why should they?"

Suzanne looked at me and responded simply, "Because the greatest gift you can give someone is the gift of the interested listener." She went on to elaborate, "A lot of these people are lonely — their children don't visit them, many are widowed, they don't have jobs, and they spend a lot of time alone. Most of them will be all too happy to talk to you — you're asking them questions about themselves, about how they live, about their homes, and about their lifestyles. Do you know how good that feels? You're giving them a gift. They will be so grateful that you are there to ask questions and listen to them. You won't have any trouble at all getting these people to talk to you."

Suzanne was right. She wasn't just right about old people — she was right about all people. Think about it. What is it we all want more than anything? We want to be heard, to be acknowledged, to have someone validate our existence, our thoughts, and our feelings. I have tested this out in many, many ways. I practice good listening skills with my friends, and they know that I love them. I listen to the men that I date, and they think I'm charming and delightful. I listen to participants in the seminars that I teach, and they think that I'm brilliant. I listen to my neighbors, and they think I'm a good problem solver. All I'm doing is providing a witness — a type of listening that conveys a message: "You're important. I care about what you think — that's why I'm listening."

When I think about all my friends, which ones do I like the most? The ones who listen to me best. In return, I try to be a good listener myself, in order to build and strengthen our friendship.

Like a bank account, friendships grow in direct proportion to interest paid. Suzanne was right ... and I'm sure glad I listened to her!

> *When we haven't the time to listen to each other's stories we seek out experts to teach us how to live. The less time we spend together at the kitchen table, the more how-to books appear in the stores and on our bookshelves. ... Because we have stopped listening to each other we may even have forgotten how to listen, stopped learning how to recognize meaning.*
>
> —Rachel Naomi Remen, M.D., author of
>   *Kitchen Table Wisdom*

Make Time for Friends

Every time we get overly busy with work and family, the first thing we do is let go of friendships with other women. We push them right to the back burner. That's really a mistake, because women are such a source of strength to each other. We nurture one another. And we need to have unpressured space in which we can do the special kind of talk that women do when they're with other women. It's a very healing experience.

> —Ruthellen Josselson, author of *Best Friends: The Pleasures and Perils of Girls' and Women's Friendships*

Everything I Need to Know about Friendship I Learned from My Women Friends

A TRUE FRIEND, FROM A TO Z...

ACCEPTS you, warts and all

BELIEVES in your potential

COMFORTS you when you're sad

DELIGHTS in your successes

EMPATHIZES with your struggles

FORGIVES you when you hurt her feelings, just as you do her

GIVES you time and attention

HUGS you ... often

INSPIRES you to do your best

JUST loves you

KEEPS your secrets

LISTENS with her heart

MAKES you want to be a better person

NEVER judges you

OCCASIONALLY disappoints you 'cause she's human, too

POINTS out your good qualities when you forget

QUESTIONS you when you're about to do something
     really dumb

RESPECTS your boundaries

SHARES her hopes and fears with you

TELLS you the truth

UNDERSTANDS you, even when you don't understand
yourself

VALUES your ideas and opinions

WILL do anything she can to help you

XTENDS a helping hand whenever you need it

YEARNS to hear from you when you're away

ZINGS with joy 'cause you're her friend

*More women ask their friends for help than
men – about 29,000 to 1.*

—Julie Hill, literary agent

Friends Tell Each Other the Truth

MY GOOD FRIEND MARGARET and I were both working for a large metropolitan newspaper – she was an executive and I was a middle manager. We had often commiserated with one another about how difficult it was to be a woman working in this "good ol' boy" organization. I had worked there a few years longer than she, and I was not holding up well under the stress. The place was really getting to me.

Margaret came into my office one day, closed the door, sat down, and after a few perfunctory pleasantries, said to me, "BJ, you either need to make your peace with this place and accept it as it is, or you need to leave. You're acting out all over the place, and people are noticing it. 'What's with BJ?' they ask. You're acting crazy. You need to snap out of it . . . or move on."

Her gaze was steady, her voice was level, and she was firm and loving at the same time. She gave me the truth, with love. It was like slapping the face of someone who is hysterical.

I was too stunned by her bluntness and her message to have a reply at the ready. All I could do was stammer and say that I would think about it.

By the next day I realized she was right. I also realized she had told me the truth with love. I was grateful and called her to tell her so. "Thanks, I needed that."

I learned a lot from that incident – I learned about truth and about love. Several years later, another woman summarized the lesson for me, "Truth without love is brutality. Love without truth is sentimentality." Margaret had told me the truth with love and I was able to hear it and understand it. She gave me an important gift. She told me the truth about my situation, and she was right — it was time for me to move on.

It's like that old cliché: "If your friends won't tell you, who will?" Margaret loved me enough to tell me the truth, and she told me in a way that let me feel the love that came along with the hard message.

What is truth without love? I can think of times when someone has said to me, "I don't want to hurt your feelings, but . . ." or, "I have your best interest at heart . . ." or, "I'm telling you this because I love you." I steel myself when I hear these words, because sometimes they simply are not true. These folks are about to drop a verbal grenade on me! I run like hell — or duck and cover my head. Like some incoming heat-seeking missile, the information they are about to give me is explosive, designed to shatter my sense of self. Their truth is brutal, because it is delivered without love.

And what is love without truth? There are some people who will withhold important information that would be helpful to me — they do so under the guise of protecting my feelings, or out of concern that I would be devastated by the truth. Sometimes they withhold the truth simply because they don't know how to tell me. Most of us are uncomfortable with telling someone we like or love something that is not pleasant. We are trained to "be nice" and "don't hurt people's feelings." So we often sacrifice the truth in our relationships (as well as in the workplace) in the name of "being nice." What we get instead is sentimental, dishonest mush!

What's the solution? My friend Margaret knows, and she taught me. It's truth with love. Thanks again, Margaret. I needed that.

What Is AUTHENTIC?

Aware

Understanding

Tactful

Honest

Empathetic

Natural

Tuned In

Intimate

Caring

Allowing Our Friends
the Dignity of Their Choices

TERI WAS IN TEARS at our monthly women's group meeting. At age forty-four, she was undergoing fertility treatments, trying to get pregnant. A couple years earlier, she had been focused intensely on her quest to find a husband. Having accomplished that a few months ago, she was now on an equally intense quest to get pregnant. So far, no luck.

The fertility treatments required that she give herself daily hormone shots, and, afraid of needles, she was freaking out. Not only that, the changes in her hormone levels were making her crazy. She was putting herself through so much stress that I wondered aloud if it was worth it. "Did you consider the possibility that maybe God doesn't want you to have a baby?" I asked gently after our meeting was over and we were alone.

The look of horror and disbelief on her face told me I had made a major blunder. I apologized instantly. "I'm so sorry. I shouldn't have said anything. It's none of my business." But it was too late – the damage was done.

By the time I got home from the meeting, Teri had left a voice-mail message telling me how hurt she was, how inappropriate my comment was, and how disappointed she was that I was so unsupportive of her quest for motherhood. My intention had been good, but the impact had been bad. What could I do?

I told Marcia, another member of our women's group, of my *faux pas.* She listened sympathetically, saying she understood my kind intentions. I was simply trying to save Teri more months of heartache by suggesting that perhaps she was on a path that was not right for her. I didn't tell her she was making a mistake — I simply inquired, raising the possibility for her to consider.

Marcia also pointed out that it really was none of my business. It's one thing if you see a friend doing something that will endanger her health or her life — like driving drunk or staying with an abusive husband. But trying to get pregnant is not a life-threatening activity — it's a personal choice. Marcia said, "We need to allow other people the dignity of their own choices."

She was right, and I am forever grateful for her succinct wisdom. Some lessons in life I have had to learn through stupid mistakes — and this was one of them! Teri has since forgiven me, and we have continued our loving friendship.

Most importantly, though, I have learned the importance of restraint of pen and tongue. Whether someone is my friend or a stranger, what they do with their personal lives is none of my business — unless it affects me (and even then, I should speak up only after careful thought and reflection).

"The dignity of personal choice" — what a wonderful concept! — the essence of free will and self-determination. I certainly want it myself, and I must allow others to have it, too.

> *If we would build on a sure foundation in friendship, we must love friends for their sake rather than for our own.*
>
> —Charlotte Brönte, British author

Hang Up That Superwoman Cape!

"I HAD TWINS IN DECEMBER 1994," Jan Leach wrote to me recently. She and I had met through mutual newspaper friends in the late 1980s, but had lost touch after I left my newspaper job in 1991. "They were seven weeks premature, and I had been on bed rest (in the hospital hooked to IVs) for seven weeks before that for pre-term labor."

Jan was now managing editor at a Midwestern newspaper, had a three-year-old at home and a husband who worked full-time. "I was having a really hellacious time being off my feet," she wrote. "I felt like my mind turned to mush, and I was highly hormonal. I wasn't allowed to work on a laptop or do anything that would stress the babies. That meant not getting out of bed. A good day was when the obstetric nurses would let me have a shower. Oh, did I mention that it was the holidays?"

I was eager to catch up on Jan's life and kept reading her letter. "Thankfully, when they were born, though they were small, the girls did quite well. After three weeks, we brought them home from the NICU. Then my life went haywire.

"Even with a daytime nanny and my own wonderful mother living with us, preemie twins were impossible to cope with. They cried constantly, had to be fed on a two-hour schedule (which left just one hour to sleep in between), needed two different formulas, different vitamins, and everything had to be color-coded. If you think one child with an ear infection is mind-numbing, think about it times two!"

I shuddered as I read Jan's story. Recalling the stress of caring for my own infant years ago, I couldn't imagine the stress of having two!

Her letter continued, "I never left the house, yet I couldn't stand the claustrophobia of demanding infants, the guilt over my three-year-old, the way I looked, everything.

"My friend Laurie Beaupre had been a rock during the hospitalization. Though I'd known her less than six months, she seemed to know instinctively that I felt out of control.

"For weeks, she would call and/or visit. She begged me to go out to lunch or shopping, anything to just get away. I had excellent excuses: doctor appointments, nanny's day off, too tired, too wired.

"One day she showed up at my house unexpected and uninvited. She announced that I had the day off and that she was taking over. She brought her own lunch, cookies for us, and a backpack. She told me I could do anything I wanted for the entire day, but I could not return until late afternoon. I tried to protest; she shooed me out of my own house.

"I called her from my driveway to ask what had gotten into her. She explained that I had to learn to say 'Yes.' This is the lesson I learned that day (I can't believe it took me nearly forty years to get it), and it's a lesson I try to remember and pass along to others.

"Women of our generation figured out we could try to have it all. We were smart, we went to school, we had careers, and we had families. We learned to be assertive not aggressive. We learned to volunteer and make a difference. We learned when to say 'No' to things that didn't matter to us personally and professionally.

"What we didn't learn was how to say 'Yes.' Yes, I need help. Yes, you can bring dinner over, sit with the kids, do my laundry, or just listen because, frankly, I can't do it all by myself. 'Yes,' I need others.

"Laurie's theory, with which I completely agree, is that we've become so professional and competent we're afraid to say 'Yes' even when people offer. And people do want to help. It's a little bit of giving back (and perhaps a small inconvenience for them). But, if you say 'Yes' it can make a big difference for just one person – *you* – today or tomorrow."

Jan is lucky to have a friend like Laurie, someone who was persistent and didn't take "No" for an answer. Laurie noticed that Jan's Superwoman cape was thinning and frayed, and saw beyond the myth of self-sufficiency that so many women have adopted. We need each other – desperately, sometimes.

I am very happy to be back in touch with Jan on a regular basis now. And I'm even happier for the lesson she taught me about friendship: that it is a matter of giving *and* receiving. It's easy to give help to others – we get to feel generous, thoughtful, and kind. Often it's harder to accept help – sometimes we feel inadequate, as if we should be Superwomen. When we accept help from our friends, we are giving them the opportunity to show how much they love us. Maybe what we need to do is say "No" to Superwoman more often, and say "Yes" to our friends instead.

Friendship and Stress

The famed Nurses' Health Study from Harvard Medical School found that the more friends women had, the less likely they were to develop physical impairments as they aged, and the more likely they were to be leading a joyful life. In fact, the results were so significant, the researchers concluded, that not having a close friend or confidante was as detrimental to your health as smoking or carrying extra weight!

That's not all — when the researchers looked at how well the women functioned after the death of their spouse, they found that even in the face of this biggest stressor of all, those women who had close friends and confidantes were more likely to survive the experience without any new physical impairment or permanent loss of vitality.

—Dr. Phyllis Silverman, Harvard University

No love, no friendship can cross the path of our destiny without leaving some mark on it forever.

—Janeen Koconis, graphic artist

God gave us our relatives.
Thank God we can choose our friends.

—Ethel Watts Mumford, humorist, novelist

3

Family:
Fun or Funky?

Ninety-eight percent of families
are dysfunctional.
The other 2 percent are lying.

—*Amy Berger, humorist, author of*
The Twenty-Year Itch

Few words generate such a range of emotions as *family.* For some of us, family evokes warm, fuzzy feelings, happy memories, and a sense of security and safety, with mental images right out of a Normal Rockwell painting. For others of us, family triggers an involuntary shudder, a knot in the pit of the stomach, and tension in the neck, with our eyeballs rolling back in our heads.

For better or for worse, your family is what it is. It's important. It's the world you were born into, with caretakers who did their jobs as best they could — very imperfectly much of the time. You undoubtedly learned a lot from your family about family — the good, the bad, and the ugly. Family is where we learn our first lessons about love … and about hate. It is where we see our first role models of what it means to be an adult. We learn about the world, about survival, about money and power, about control and compassion, and so much more. Family is where our learning begins … and the learning never ends.

Structure Is Love

"WHAT TIME DO I HAVE TO COME HOME?" I would ask my mom as I headed out the door after dinner. My homework was done, and I was eager to spend time with my friends at the Teen Club. The Teen Club, right next door to the school, had pool tables, a jukebox, and lots of sofas and chairs for lounging – it was the place where all of us junior high kids hung out.

"Be home by ten," my mother replied.

"Awwwww, Mommmm," I whined. "All the other kids get to stay out later ... why do I have to come home so early?" Thus would begin our nightly argument. Sometimes Dad would join in, but more often he stayed out of it. He was the "big gun" who stayed in the background most of the time, unless I harangued my mother too much.

Mom and I would argue for a few minutes, then I would make a big dramatic scene as I left the apartment, making sure I closed the front door with a *thump* just for emphasis. "Parents are so unreasonable!" I thought to myself as I stormed off to the Teen Club.

I was always home on time, but I wasn't gracious about it. I whined and pouted. I slumped and slouched. I had many different ways of expressing my pubescent displeasure with my Neanderthal parents.

Then came the fateful night. As I headed out the door, I asked the same old question, "What time do I have to come home?"

My mother dropped the bombshell: "Oh, come home whenever you like. You've got a house key."

I couldn't believe my ears: "You mean, no curfew tonight?"

"Nope. You're a big girl," my mother explained. "You can stay out as long as you like. We don't care when you come home. We're going to bed. Just be quiet when you come in." Dad, as usual, was silent.

I was ecstatic! I couldn't believe my good fortune. I skipped out the door, free at last!

The days rolled by, and my parents pretty much ignored me each evening as I headed out the door. No curfew. I could do whatever I wanted.

Then something weird happened. The freedom they granted me started to bother me. Something was missing. I felt a little lost . . . alone . . . cast adrift in my teen activities. By the end of the week, I was in tears.

"You don't love me anymore!" I sobbed after dinner. "You don't care about me! How could you not care when I come home?" I accused them.

My mother gave my dad a knowing smile, then turned to me calmly and said, "Okay, be home by ten o'clock."

Suddenly, everything was all right again. I was reassured. They did love me. They did care about what happened to me at night. It felt good to have a boundary.

My mother has always been skillful at teaching me lessons by experience. Somehow she knew that kids learn much better by experiencing things than by someone telling them things. She also knew that loving your kids doesn't mean letting them do whatever they want — it means giving them boundaries and guide-lines within which to live and grow.

To this day, whenever I go visit Mom, I still try to be home by ten o'clock.

"What are you thinking about, my dear?"
"Nothing, Mother."
An excellent answer.
The same I invariably gave when I was her age.

—Colette, French writer

If I knew then what I know now about parenting,
I'd have stayed a virgin.

—Lillian Carter (mother to President Jimmy Carter and his rascal brother Billy Carter)

Mothers and Holidays

Every Fourth of July I call my mom and wish her a happy birthday. It's not her birthday – it's mine. But I tell her, "You did all the work, Mom. All I had to do was show up!" We both laugh and she tells me again about the day I was born, relating all the little details as if they happened just last week. I listen as if I'm hearing all this for the first time, even though I've heard it dozens of times before.

The Fourth of July is the holiday I most associate with my mother. She and one of my dad's cousins were both pregnant at the same time, and both were due to deliver their babies on July 4th. It was jokingly considered "a race" in our family to see which young mom would deliver first. Ever punctual, Mom was right on time. My cousin's mom was late – her baby came on July 5th. I must confess, I always felt just a teensy bit superior to my cousin for that fact – and proud of Mom for winning the race.

So, every year I call and thank her for all her hard work giving birth to me on the Fourth of July. She gave me life and I came into her life with a bang!

Do you associate a particular holiday with your mother?

Christmas?	Hanukkah?
Thanksgiving?	Cinco de Mayo?
Easter?	All Saint's Day?
New Years?	Ramadan?
St. Patrick's Day?	Valentine's Day?
Labor Day?	Memorial Day?
President's Day?	Martin Luther King, Jr.'s birthday?
Kwanzaa?	Chinese New Year?
Yom Kippur?	Rosh Hashanah?
Buddha's birthday?	Ground Hog Day?
Halloween?	Dia de los Muertos?
Others?	

We Sometimes Hurt the Ones We Love

HEATHER MOVED TO CALIFORNIA IN 1992 from a small town in Vermont. Shortly after her move, she invited her mother to come out and visit her in her new home. Her mom came for two weeks, and they had a wonderful time, visiting all the wonderful sights of San Francisco, traveling up to the wine country for a day trip, and doing a bit of mother/daughter shopping.

Several years went by, and Heather missed her mom. She called her one day and said, "Gee, Mom, it's been a few years since you came out to California. Maybe you'd like to come out for a visit again?"

Her mom replied, "Oh, but I've already seen San Francisco."

Heather was hurt. I could still hear a faint trace of pain in her voice when she told me this story ten years later.

Her mom was not a mean woman; she was just emotionally cool and aloof, "in that Northeast kind of manner," as Heather described her. She had been a good caretaker for her children. "She was rather like a Pilgrim living in a modern age – hardworking, polite, sweet, and honest," Heather said. But there wasn't much in the way of emotional intimacy between mother and daughter – although there was love.

"I couldn't believe what my mother said to me that day," Heather told me. "As if the only reason she should come to California was to see the sights. She was totally oblivious to the fact that I wanted her to come see me."

Heather's story made me think of times that my own mother had inadvertently hurt her children's feelings. I recall her birthday about twelve years ago. We were gathered around the dinner table, eating birthday cake while Mom happily opened her gifts. As she opened a package from my brother, her face fell in disappointment. "Floor mats!" she blurted out. "I don't want floor mats! Take 'em back – I wanted an electric blanket!" I looked at my brother and could see the pain on his face, as he stoically took the package from her and set it aside. He thought floor mats for her new car would be the perfect present and that she would be pleased. My heart hurt for him. I wanted to shake my mother. What was she thinking!?

In listening to Heather, I wondered how often I had hurt my own child's feelings. I can't think of any incidents, but I'll bet he can. I shudder to think about it.

Heather's experience with her mom reminded me of the power of words – how hurtful they can be, and how once spoken, we can never take them back. Sometimes there is a huge gap between the *intent* of a comment and its *impact.* As a mother, a sister, a daughter, a niece, and an aunt, I am responsible for my own communication with my family members. I need to gauge the listening of the other person, and speak into their listening if I want to avoid hurting them. It's easy to forget how sensitive my family members are – to unthinkingly hurt the ones I love the most. I learned something important from Heather's mom's mistake: I must speak more often from my heart, and less from my head.

I was on a corner the other day when a wild-looking sort of gypsy-looking lady with a dark veil over her face grabbed me right on Ventura Boulevard and said, "Karen Haber! You're never going to find happiness, and no one is ever going to marry you." I said, "Mom, leave me alone."

—Karen Haber, comedienne

If it's not one thing, it's your mother.

—Gilda Radner, comedienne

How are we to be the mothers we want our daughters to have, if we are still sorting out who our own mothers are and what they mean to us?

—Letty Cottin Pogrebin, author of *Growing Up Free*

The Changing American Family

1970	1995
Married couples with children made up 40 percent of households.	Married couples with children made up 25 percent of households.
There were 3.14 people per household.	There were 2.65 people per household.
1 out of every 5 households had five or more people.	1 out of every 10 households had five or more people.
People living alone made up one-sixth of households.	People living alone made up one-fourth of the households.
5.6 million families were maintained by women with no husband present.	12.2 million families were maintained by women with no husband present.
1.2 million families were maintained by men with no wife present.	3.2 million families were maintained by men with no wife present.
2 out of 3 households were in metropolitan areas.	4 out of 5 households were in metropolitan areas.
44 percent of families had no own children under 18 at home.	1 percent of families had no own children under 18 at home.

Note: A "household" is an individual or a group of people who occupy a housing unit, whereas a "family" is a group of two or more people, one of whom is the householder, living together, who are related by birth, marriage, or adoption.

(Source: U.S. Census Bureau)

Dear BJ,

My mother and her sister haven't spoken to each other in thirty years — a fact that pains me because I love them both very much and I think they're stubbornly missing out on something important. About ten years ago, "Dear Abby" wrote a column about Forgiveness Week, with a lovely story about family forgiveness. I cut out the article and sent photocopies of it to each of them. Then I waited.

When I next spoke to my mother, I asked her what she thought of the piece. She said, "It was nice," and changed the subject.

Then I got an angry letter from my aunt. "Your grandmother was a boor, your mother is a boor, and you are rapidly becoming one yourself!" she wrote. "Butt out! It's none of your business!" I didn't hear from her again for many months.

Ouch! Did I learn a painful lesson! Since then, I have accepted the fact that I have to let family members work out their own problems. I can't make things happy for everyone, as much as I would like to. If they choose to be mad at each other for decades, that is their choice. It's also their loss. But the best I can do is just take care of my own relationships within my family, and let others do the same.

Sadder but wiser,
Louise Francette Malveaux

"Home" is any four walls that enclose the right person.

—Helen Rowland, author of
Reflections of a Bachelor Girl

At midlife I'm having to recognize that there are people I may never be reconciled with. people I loved dearly but we went as far as we could go together. we loved; we tried; that may have to be enough.

—zana, poet, artist, author of *herb womon*

The Daughters I Never Had

I'VE LEARNED A LOT FROM the girls and women my son Michael has dated over the past fifteen years. Each of them reminded me of myself at certain points in my life, and each of them taught me something.

Beth, the girl that Michael fell in love with in high school, was like a skittish little fawn. She was shy and insecure, pretty and petulant – very much a child/woman who had not yet come into her own. She triggered new feelings in me – strong maternal feelings for someone I had just met. I wanted to mother her, to reassure her that she was loved and cared about, and to help her grow more self-confident and secure. I was surprised at these powerful motherly feelings I had for her, since I had always been quite content to have a son and had never before felt this longing to mother a daughter. On some deep level, perhaps I sensed that Beth was a girl who needed a mother; her own family background was pretty dismal. Her parents had been divorced and remarried to multiple partners. Beth had been through umpteen stepmoms over the years, and hadn't lived with her biological mother since she was a toddler. She was a wounded little spirit. Over the four years that she and my son were together, I gradually became the mom that she never had, and she became the daughter that I never had. She still sends me a card on Mother's Day every year.

Rikki came next, about nine months after Beth and Michael broke up. She was fiercely independent – a bit of a wild child. She had dropped out of high school at sixteen, traveled to Europe with a band, and had developed a variety of skills for supporting herself: cutting hair, playing in the band, designing and sewing cool clothes, freelancing as a photographer, and other assorted odd jobs. She was the epitome of resourcefulness and self-reliance, with street smarts honed by years of being on her own. I liked and admired Rikki. I appreciated her ability to take care of herself in the world and the creative way she pieced together a living and a lifestyle, providing her with optimum freedom and flexibility. She and Michael were a couple for two years, during which time I became the mom that she never had. With Beth and Rikki, now I had two "daughters."

The third one was Meriel, not a girl but a woman in her thirties, who was seven years older than Michael. They spent six years together and ultimately got married. When Michael first met her, he came home and said, "You're going to really like her, Mom. She's just like you — beautiful, smart, artistic, articulate, a feminist, and controlling." "What?" I yelped. "Me, controlling?" Ooh, the truth hurts sometimes. But he was right, and Meriel was yet another version of me.

All three of these young women were like mirrors in which I could see reflections of parts of my past and my personality. They helped me see aspects of myself that I didn't want to own. They demonstrated how powerful a mother is in the life and mind of her son, and how, for better or for worse, a mother is arguably the single most important influence on a child's future. I learned that men (as well as women) often date and marry someone who represents one of their parents, usually the one with whom they still have the most unresolved issues.

Finally, I learned that I still do have that leftover mothering energy for a daughter. There are many wonderful experiences and adventures that can only be shared and appreciated between females. Beth, Rikki, and Meriel are the three daughters I never had, and I am grateful for all that I learned from them. Thank you, girls.

In our society it is acceptable to blame Mom. Then add the Perfect Mother and Bad Mother images, which lead us to blame Mom for not being perfect when she doesn't live up to our idealized image, and, when she does something not so terrific, to blame her for being horrible rather than only human. In view of the intense social pressure placed on girls to be "little mothers," it is troubling that their most salient model is not regarded as a worthy one.

—Paula Caplan, author of *Don't Blame Mother*

The more you love your children, the more shocked they are to discover that you possess a single strand of ambivalent — or negative — feeling. Insatiable for this love we expect to be absolute, we cannot forgive its mere humanness.

—Marilyn French, author of *Her Mother's Daughter*

That reflexive maternal guilt . . . emerges at the infant's first wail: "I'm sorry. I'm sorry. . . . I'm sorry I can't keep you perfectly full, perfectly dry, perfectly free from gas and fear, perfectly, perfectly happy."

—Nancy Mairs, author of *Plaintext: Deciphering a Woman's Life*

Elvis Turkey

My daughter-in-law, Meriel, has a thing for Elvis – she watches his old movies, listens to his music, has Elvis knickknacks around the house, and even has a bust of Elvis surrounded by candles in the living room (she calls it her Elvis Shrine). The wedding ring she had made for my son was a horseshoe-shaped ring, covered in pave diamonds, just like one that Elvis wore. And their wedding cake was an exact replica of the cake from Elvis' and Priscilla's wedding. Meriel just loves anything that has to do with Elvis.

One Thanksgiving, I made the turkey and stuffing for our dinner together, using a recipe that my mother had handed down to me. The stuffing called for a cup of melted Crisco, and the turkey was basted with Crisco every 20-30 minutes as well. Needless to say, it was a tasty bird, slathered with all that shortening, making the turkey skin brown and crispy. When Meriel complimented me on the turkey and stuffing, I told her about the Crisco. "An Elvis turkey!" she exclaimed (referring to Elvis' fondness for fatty foods later in his life – his weight ballooning to an all-time high). The "Elvis turkey" name stuck, and that's what we've called it ever since. I croon to the turkey as I'm basting it, "Love me tender, love me true...."

Elvis Turkey

Ingredients and Quantities

Turkey weight	4 lb.	6 lb.	10 lb.	12 lb.	20 lb.
Soft bread cubes	6 cups	9 cups	15 cups	1 ⅛ gal.	2 gal.
or number of bread slices	6	9	15	18	30
Crisco	¼ cup	⅓ cup	½ cup	⅔ cup	1 cup
Broth or water	⅓ cup	⅔ cup	1 cup	1 ⅓ cups	2 cups
Chopped onion	½ cup	⅔ cup	1 cup	1 ⅓ cups	2 cups
Chopped celery	½ cup	⅔ cup	1 cup	1 ⅓ cups	2 cups
Poultry seasoning	1 ⅓ tsp.	2 tsp.	1 Tbsp.	1 ⅓ Tbsp.	2 Tbsp.
Salt and pepper	⅔ tsp.	1 tsp.	1 ½ tsp.	2 tsp.	1 Tbsp.

Olives – 1 or 2 cans of small or medium black olives, depending on amount of stuffing

Sausage (the kind you make into patties) – ½ lb. to 1 lb., depending on amount of stuffing

Dill weed – ⅓ to ½ tsp., to taste

Directions

Slice bread into crouton-sized pieces (I use half white bread and half wheat).

Chop onions and celery and boil in saucepan with water to cover; cook till tender.

Fry one-half pound (or more to taste) sausage so that it is crumbly, like ground beef.

Drain juice from canned black olives.

Cook turkey neck and giblets in big saucepan of water (slightly salted) – about ½ hour for liver and 2-2½ hours for neck and gizzard – and use this broth for the stuffing.

continued

Put chopped bread into very large mixing bowl or big pan.

Add dry ingredients: salt and pepper, dill weed, and poultry seasoning.

Add sausage and olives; start mixing the stuffing.

Add wet ingredients: cooked onion and celery, broth, and melted Crisco.

Mix well, either with a big spoon or your hands.

Stuff the turkey; then put any additional stuffing in a baking casserole dish with lid; bury the turkey neck in the dish of dressing to give it more turkey flavor; cook at 350 degrees F for 30-60 minutes, depending on amount.

Cover turkey and bake according to weight, basting every 20-30 minutes with Crisco.

Be sure to make gravy from the grease and turkey juice in the bottom of the baking pan, and serve it with the turkey and stuffing. Elvis wouldn't have it any other way!

Advice to Mother of the Groom

1. Wear beige

and

2. Keep your mouth shut.

(Source: Judy Wilson, Public Affairs Officer, Army Corps of Engineers)

Who Controls the Family Purse Strings?

MY STEPMOTHER KAREN AND I had had a lovely afternoon, one of those "girls' day out" kind of things. We had lunch at a wonderful café, visited some charming boutiques, and finished our afternoon off with a movie. We had a great time. I often think Karen is more like my sister than my stepmom. We have similar tastes, interests, and outgoing personalities – and because she is eighteen years younger than Dad, she is closer to my age than to his. We have become good friends over the years.

We drove back to the condo where she and Dad live. As she got out of the car, Karen took several of her packages from the back seat and put them in the trunk. She had just one small shopping bag in her hand, which she was going to take into the house. As I got out of the car, I said, "I think I'll put my purchases in my car, so I don't have to take them into the house and then into the car later. I'll save myself some work." What I really meant was, "I'm going to put my bags in my car so that Dad won't see them. I don't want him to know I spent any money." Karen and I were both on the same wavelength, and we each knew it.

Dad is from the Depression Generation, and he has always been frugal. I tease him, "Dad, they don't have luggage racks on hearses, you know!" He replies, "If I can't take it with me, I'm not going!" and we laugh. His thriftiness is a quality that has both good aspects and bad. The upside of his frugality is that he always has money in savings for emergencies; he doesn't lose sleep over debt; all his bills and taxes get paid on time; and he feels secure that he has plenty of money to see him out — he won't outlive his savings! The downside is that he worries about not getting the best possible deal; he sometimes hesitates on investments too long, fearful of losing money, and then misses the opportunity entirely. Sometimes his children suspect that he doesn't love them enough because he doesn't want to spend money on their desires.

Is my dad the only man in the world like this? Are Karen and I the only two women who hide purchases from the men in their lives? What's the story here?

I learned the answer to these and other important questions about families and money in a fascinating book I read called *Women Who Shop Too Much* by Carolyn Wesson. In it, she includes a chapter on why women hide their purchases, and how money and control issues are intertwined. She also writes about how many women get their intimacy needs met by the sales clerks in the boutiques they frequent, who flatter and fawn over them, solicitous of every desire and fantasy. Another chapter explains how women use shopping as a way to express creativity, buying colorful clothes, décor for the home, and pretty things to make life more appealing. The overall theme of the book highlights how millions of women use shopping as a way of nurturing themselves, filling inner emotional needs that aren't met by their husbands, lovers, and families.

How women and men handle their money speaks volumes about their families: whether or not they feel loved, how they provide for their children, and ways in which they act out their relationships with other family members. Money is intertwined with issues of power, control, sex, self-esteem, love, and loyalty. Carolyn Wesson's book showed me that hiding purchases is just one small example of how interpersonal issues show up in the family checkbook.

The most important thing I learned from *Women Who Shop Too Much* is how important it is for families to take the mystery out of money. I remember when I was a teenager asking my mother how much money Dad made. "That's none of your business," she replied. Money is the last taboo, it seems. People today will talk about their sex lives, their dysfunctional families, their alcohol and drug problems, their abusive relationships, their illnesses and bodies, even their struggles with God — but talk of money is still *verboten.* Enough already. It's high time we bring money out of the proverbial closet.

Nothing cheers a girl up like shopping.

—Madonna, singer, actress

Dear BJ,

Advice to children can be risky, and as ours matured we had a creed we adhered to:

- Never give adult children advice unless they are asking for money.

- If adult children ask for advice, that's another story.

It worked for us.

But in their developmental years advice was needed — after all, that's what parenting is all about.

Regards,

Virginia Quirk (mother of eight children)

Which Is Your FAMILY?

Fulfilling		Frustrating
Affirming		Annoying
Meaningful	*or*	Mean
Insightful		Infuriating
Loving		Lunatic
Yardstick to grow by		Yelling

Or is it *both*?

Welcome Home the Prodigal Son!

THERE ARE FEW THINGS in family life more painful than estrangement. And there is probably no estrangement more painful than one between parent and child. My friend Leah knows this only too well.

She was blessed with two wonderful sons, Ari and Gil, both of whom she adored. They were handsome, smart, creative boys who started to change and grow apart as they got older. Ari was the more traditional son, graduating from college, starting a career, having a family, and enjoying a good relationship with his parents. Gil, on the other hand, joined a cult in his early twenties and cut himself off from his parents and brother. Leah was confused, frightened, and heartbroken.

She and I first met about eighteen years ago, a year or two after Gil had joined this cult. Leah was frantically doing research on cults, talking to anyone who knew anything about them, wondering whether or how she could convince her son to leave the cult, and otherwise tearing her hair out with grief. My own son was around eleven or twelve at the time, and I never thought that he would grow up and join a cult, but then, neither had Leah. I shuddered to think of the uncertainty involved in raising children – you never can tell what'll happen.

As the years went by, Leah had to accept the fact that her son was gone from her life, perhaps forever. Her grief softened, but the flicker of hope was never extinguished. Occasionally, Gil would surface. She heard from him when her father (Ari and Gil's grandfa-ther) died, although he didn't come to the funeral. When his father (Leah's ex-husband) died, Gil did attend that funeral. He also came to his grandmother's funeral, but didn't stick around for long.

Every once in a while, Gil would communicate with his brother Ari, and Leah would hear the latest news secondhand. Those were always bittersweet messages — she was glad to hear that he was alive and doing fine, but it also reminded her of what she was missing.

Then one day, a miracle happened. Gil called Leah to tell her that he was getting married to a Danish woman and the wedding would be in Copenhagen. Would Leah please come to the wedding? She was ecstatic! She would have said "Yes" even if the wedding was on Mars! She called me to share the good news. We rejoiced together — two mothers of sons celebrating new hope.

She went to the wedding, which was last year, and it was won-derful. Not only was she reunited with her son, she also got a lov-ing, beautiful, compassionate daughter-in-law. Her happiness knew no bounds.

A few months later, the September 11 terrorist attack took place, and Leah was terrified that once again she had lost her son, who was now living with his new family in Virginia, near the Pen-tagon. After having been estranged for almost twenty years, Leah was afraid that terrorists had cruelly snatched Gil from her, just months after their reconciliation. She called and sent e-mails for hours on end and was finally able to find out that Gil was okay. It was days before she was able to make contact with him directly, since he was working around the clock as a volunteer, helping his neighbors cope with the crisis. She was able to speak daily with her daughter-in-law, who calmed her nerves. Her new relationship with Gil seemed delicate and fragile – she was still nervous that some twist of fate might take him from her again.

Just before Thanksgiving, Gil called Leah and asked her if she would like to come to Virginia to celebrate the holiday. She agreed eagerly, and journeyed east to spend an especially grateful Thanksgiving with her son and his new wife. During that visit she had an opportunity to learn more about the "lost" years and reflect on the upright, loving, responsible young man who had emerged.

Leah also realized something important that weekend – one person's "cult" is another person's chosen life path. Their holiday dinner included some of Gil's friends from those "lost years," and Leah was amazed that they weren't at all what she expected – they were intelligent, warm, kind, funny, and creative. "If these are the kind of people my son has spent the past twenty years with," she told me, "then I have to reconsider everything I thought about his lifestyle."

Leah and I were reminiscing recently about how things had changed in our lives over the many years we have known one another. I marveled at the miracle that had brought Gil back into her life. She doesn't know why he came back or why his hard heart softened – and she doesn't care. She is just grateful that he is back in her life. Her prodigal son has returned, and that's all that matters.

Leah's experience taught me two things: (1) Our children sometimes choose paths that we don't understand or approve of, but we must accept their right to choose for themselves; and (2) Miracles can happen, even in the toughest of family situations, even after long estrangements. Healing is possible, forgiveness is granted, and love does its best to make up for lost time.

> *Looking back to find the discarded pieces of the original Mother, we find our answers and we bring our own birth mothers back to us, brush them off, give them warm baths, hot tea, and heal their stories.*
>
> —Zella Bardsley, writer, artist, teacher

Four nice little old ladies get together for their weekly bridge game:

"Oy," sighs the first, as she settles into her chair.

"Oy vey," nods the second as she adjusts her sweater.

"Oy vey iz meir," mutters the third as she sets her purse on the floor.

"Girls, that's enough about the children," says the fourth. "Let's play bridge."

4

Making Peace with the Past

Childhood is the first inescapable political
situation each of us has to negotiate.
You are powerless. You are on the wrong
side in every respect. Besides that,
there's the size thing.

—*June Jordan, poet, novelist, critic*

The past is a weird thing. Somehow it keeps showing up in the present. Even worse, sometimes it seems to predict the future! Old issues that we thought were finished show up disguised with new faces. Old wounds get reopened by new people ... or sometimes by the same people who gave us the original wounds. Our fathers show up in our relationships with men. We're haunted by the fear that we might be turning into our mothers. Old parental issues get reenacted with authority figures like bosses. What's the deal here? More importantly, is there anything we can do about it?

A wise friend once told me that "until you get complete with your parents, you can't get complete with anyone." Her advice was this: If you have unresolved issues with your parents, drop everything else you're doing and take care of that. If you don't, then old garbage from the past will continue to clutter up your life and your relationships forever.

I believe my friend. I think she's right. It's time to get the past out of the present and put it back in the past where it belongs. It's time to open up the future to new freedom and new possibilities.

Recovering from Childhood

ONCE IN A VERY GREAT WHILE, I read a book that hits me like a ton of bricks. It's happened maybe half a dozen times in my life so far — reading a book that has a watershed effect on the whole rest of my life. *The Drama of the Gifted Child,* by German psychiatrist Alice Miller, was such a book. It was published in the United States in 1981, having been previously published in Germany under the title *Prisoner of Childhood.* Jack, the man I was passionately in love with at the time, gave me a copy. "It reminded me of you," he said simply when he handed it to me. It's a slim little paperback, and I read it over a weekend. By the time I was finished, I was curled up in the fetal position on my bed, sobbing with grief. That Jack, always the master of the understatement! No wonder the book reminded him of me — Alice Miller had written the story of my childhood.

Apparently it is the story of many people's childhoods, because the book has sold more than 800,000 copies and is still in print some twenty years after publication.

Miller's thesis is this: All children are born gifted, full of raw potential for creativity, curiosity, discovery, and invention. The parents' job is to provide a mirror for the gifted child, so that the child can see herself in her parents' loving eyes. The parents are to serve as validating witnesses to the blossoming of their child, from a tiny bud of pure potential to a fully formed flower of accomplishment and achievement. The problem is, most parents didn't receive this kind of nurturing from *their* parents, so they are still trying to get their own psychic needs met, and therefore are unavailable to the child who needs their attention so much. Thus, the child is wounded, grows up hungry for the mirroring and validation she needed, and spends the rest of her life trying to find what she didn't get as a child.

This theory explains why so many women grow up and marry someone like their fathers, and why so many men grow up and marry someone like their mothers. We grow up emotionally stunted, and because of our wounds, we go in search of the parent we wanted and needed but never had. It's like having a tooth missing in your mouth – your tongue keeps going back, again and again, to touch the gap where your tooth should be. It's instinctive; it's subconscious.

Miller points out that we can never go back in time and fill that void. We can't make up now for what we didn't get as children. If we insist on trying, we end up neglecting our own children in the process, and the same drama gets passed on to another generation. We perpetuate the same wounds on them that our parents inflicted on us.

Miller says that all there is to do is face the fact of your childhood as it was, mourn the loss of what might have been, grieve, and then move on. Simple to say, hard to do.

Miller's book was helpful in giving me a framework for understanding my own childhood and for seeing that I was doing the exact same thing to my own child. The grief I felt was overwhelming. I cried; I walked about in sadness for days after reading her book. But it was good – it was the beginning of a long, slow healing process. In finally giving up the myth that I would find perfect parental love in a man, I could move on with my life and begin to heal those wounds once and for all. I still had time to try to be a better mother to my young son so that he might feel a little less wounded when time came for him to recover from his own childhood.

Recovering from childhood wounds has meant growing out of my emotional immaturity and becoming willing to be an adult. As it says in the Bible, it was time to "put aside childish things" and finally grow up. I am definitely a late bloomer in that regard, but better late than not at all.

Learn to get in touch with the silence within yourself and know that everything in this life has a purpose. There are no mistakes, no coincidence, all events are blessings given to us to learn from.

—Elizabeth Kübler-Ross, psychiatrist, expert on
  death and dying

We all live in suspense from day to day; in other words, you are the hero of your own story.

—Mary McCarthy, author of *On the Contrary*

Dear BJ,

I guess I was complaining but didn't even realize it. My mother and I were doing dishes, and I was telling her how I felt about our Easter together. It was lovely spending the day with her and her second husband and his children, but deep inside me a little voice kept whispering, "If only Papa were here, the holiday would be complete." When I told her this, she looked at me with that tough-love look of hers and said, "You need to accept the fact that our family is never going to be the way it was before."

I didn't say anything; I wiped my hands on a towel and left the kitchen.

On my way home that evening, the truth hit me: What I really needed to do was accept the fact that my family never was the way I wanted them to be ... even when Mama and Papa were together! I was still clinging to this fantasy family in my head – a family that never existed.

Mama was right, I did need to let go of the hope of us being one big happy family. I needed to accept my family as they were – both my past family and my present one. A hard realization, but an important one.

Sign me,
Realistically yours,
Carmen Ruiz

How Do You FORGIVE?

Feel your hurt.

Open your mind.

Release your anger.

Give love a chance.

Inquire within your heart.

Venture into dialogue.

Embrace the other person.

Nudge yourself to keep at it,
   even when you don't want to.

Enjoy new possibilities and freedom.

Seek Divine guidance and help.

Savor your new serenity and peace.

Forgiveness is the key to action and freedom.

—Hannah Arendt, philosopher

Am I My Mother's Daughter?

HOW MANY OF US ARE SECRETLY (or not so secretly) haunted by the fear that we're turning into our mothers? The thought has crossed my mind more than a few times.

My brother loves to tease me by pointing out all the ways I am like my mother. "The apple doesn't fall too far from the tree, ya know," he smirks. He knows this freaks me out. My son does the same thing. Last time we went to visit my mother together, my son sat in the big easy chair, chuckling softly as he watched my mother go about her daily activities. I knew what he was thinking. "What are you laughing at?" I asked in mock irritation.

"You do the same thing as Grandma!" he laughed.

"I do not!" I huffed defensively. I knew he was right, but I was not going to admit it.

So here's the question: Why does it bother me to acknowledge similarities between my mother and me? And why do these mother/daughter similarities seem to bother so many other women as well? I know I'm not alone in this.

I recall a Life History class I taught at USC's Gerontology Center. One week, I gave my students the assignment to "Write about your life's work." The next week, students shared their writing assignments in class. One woman spoke up with a very serious look on her face: "You know, before I took this class, if anyone had asked me about my life's work, I would have told them I was a lab technician. That's what I'm paid to do, and that's what my training was in – lab work. But as I wrote on this assignment, I realized what my real life's work is – my real life's work is proving that I am not my mother."

"Proving it to whom?" I asked her.

"Proving it to the world . . . ," she replied. "No . . . maybe proving it to myself.

"So, did you prove it?" I asked.

"No," she replied. "In writing this assignment, I realized that I've been wrong all these years. I'm at a time in my life when I need to come to terms with my mother – and my father as well, for that matter. I see now that I am my mother's daughter, and I'm at peace with it. I can accept her just the way she is, and just the way she isn't. I've finally given up wanting my mother to be something that she isn't. For the first time, I feel like I can love her and accept her just as she is."

"That's pretty remarkable," I replied.

"Well, you want to know something else?" She continued, "Something even more important came out of this. In accepting my mother the way she is, I finally feel like I can accept myself too – just the way I am!" Her face lit up with a smile, as she handed me her assignment.

Ah, that's one of the joys of being a teacher. You get to learn from your students. That student taught me that when we come to accept our parents and love them for who they are, warts and all, there is enormous freedom and healing available in that moment.

It probably made her mom pretty happy, too!

The delights of self-discovery are always available.

—Gail Sheehy, author of *Passages*

Emotional Inheritance Is a Mixed Bag

MY FRIEND ARLEEN AND I occasionally get together over sushi when I am in her area. I don't see her as often as I'd like because we live 100-plus miles apart, but when we get together we pick up right where we left off in our last conversation. Our talk always comes around to the subject of kids, since we both have adult children (she has four and I have one). Like many mothers, we have discovered that our adorable kids have grown up into harsh critics.

"How's your son?" she asked me at our last dinner.

"He's fine, I think," I reply. "But I'm not really sure, because I haven't seen him in a few weeks. He's avoiding me."

"Why?" Arleen asks.

"He says I'm impossible," I shrug. "No matter what I say or do, it always seems to be wrong. He is so critical of me...."

"My son, too," she nods knowingly. "He has this laundry list of all the things I did wrong as his mother. And he never misses an opportunity to tell me what he thinks."

Arleen starts wagging her chopsticks at me, like a reproachful finger. "But I have an answer for him," she continues. "'Just remember, David,'" I say, 'that the same place you got all the bad stuff you're *kvetching* about is where you got all the good stuff too!'"

"What a great response!" I laugh. "I'm gonna remember that!"

I love Arleen so much. She's like the Jewish mother I might have had if I'd been Jewish! She is smart and savvy, and doesn't take nonsense from anyone, even her kids. She loves them dearly, but doesn't hesitate to draw the line when they get out of hand. I'm grateful to have the opportunity to learn from her.

I am much kinder to my own mother these days, because I know that I inherited some wonderful qualities from her: generosity, spontaneity, creativity, curiosity, flexibility, and the ability to look at change as an adventure. Yes, I inherited some things I would prefer not to have — but the good far outweighs the bad.

My only hope is that someday my son will recognize that about me!

When one is a stranger to oneself, then one is estranged from others too.

—Anne Morrow Lindbergh, aviator, writer

Emotional Balance Sheet

Accountants make balance sheets, listing both assets and liabilities. It's a useful device, the balance sheet. I started one for myself, and here are some of the things I have listed so far:

ASSETS I INHERITED	LIABILITIES I INHERITED
From Mom	**From Mom**
Curiosity	Overly sensitive
Generosity	Too impulsive
Flexibility	Inconsistency
Homebody	Hermit-like tendencies
Concern for others	Codependency
Helpfulness	Bossiness
"Nesting" skills	
Optimism	
Kindness	
Care about appearance	
Friendliness	
Creativity	
From Dad	**From Dad**
Confidence	Arrogance
Ambition and drive	Too goal-oriented
Good looks	Critical of others
Charm and social skills	Manipulative, sometimes
High standards	Perfectionist
Skill with words	Verbally hurtful
High intelligence	Disdainful of dumb people
Quick thinker	Impatience
Enjoyment of travel	
Sense of adventure	
Leadership skills	
Strong work ethic	

Make an emotional balance sheet for yourself. What qualities, abilities, and skills did you inherit from your parents? What are you grateful for? What are some of the less-than-wonderful characteristics you inherited? What can you do about them?

Character is what you know you are, not what others think you have.

—Marva Collins, educator, school reformer

It's Time to Let Parents off the Hook

HAVE YOU EVER HEARD SOMEONE say something so simple and yet so profound that you were stunned at its truth? One of my mother's statements prompted this reaction from me.

At the time, I had been complaining a lot about the parenting I had received from my folks. In my opinion, they were too strict, controlling, perfectionist, rigid, and so on. I viewed myself as the helpless victim of their less-than-enlightened parenting practices. I felt that the problems I had as an adult were the direct result of the dysfunctional family in which I grew up ... or so I thought. I had plenty of blame to heap upon my mom and dad.

In the middle of one of my grievance litanies, my mother turned to me and said simply, "Blame your parents for the way you are; blame yourself if you stay that way." Then she turned back to washing the dishes.

The statement was like a glass of cold water in my face. If I had had my wits about me, I would have said, "Thanks, Mom, I needed that." But I didn't have my wits about me. I was stunned into silence.

Today I am grateful for my mother's comment. It took me a while to come to grips with the enormity of it ... I had to digest and reflect upon the implications of her message. She was right. I could, indeed, blame my parents for the mistakes they had made and the kind of person I grew up to be. Nothing in her statement implied that my parents were not accountable for their actions.

But I also had a choice. I could choose to continue to wallow in victimhood and blame the past for my problems today. Or, I could take responsibility for my future — I could choose to change. I can resign myself to the fact that "character is fate." Or, I can take the stance that human beings can change, rather dramatically when they want to.

I chose to change and adopted my mother's statement as my mantra. Today, I am a work in progress, and my future is limited only by my own beliefs and my willingness to work on myself. Mom was right . . . I have only myself to blame if I stay stuck in the past.

A woman sees what she looks for.

—**Barbara Jenkins, author**

Lightening the Load

Everyone has "baggage" – guilt, hurt, resentment, regrets, disappointments, unresolved conflicts, betrayals, misunderstandings, and fears. Some people have big steamer trunks of unfinished business, others have matched sets of baggage, and some just have fanny packs. It doesn't matter how much or how little baggage you hold onto – what matters is what it's doing to you. How does it affect your peace of mind? Your relationships? Your health? How much longer do you want to carry that stuff around with you?

Here are some suggestions for letting go of some of your baggage:

- Get professional help from a reputable therapist or counselor.
- Participate in twelve-step groups like Codependents Anonymous (CODA), Adult Children of Alcoholics (ACA), Al-Anon, and others.
- Attend self-help seminars or join a support group.
- Read self-help books; put into practice what you learn.
- Adopt spiritual practices; seek spiritual guidance.
- Design rituals and ceremonies that enable you to let go.
- Practice forgiveness – start small, work up to the bigger things.
- Write letters to the person you're upset with (even if they're dead), and then burn the letters.

continued

- Make art that helps you work out your past pain (paint, make collages, do pottery).
- Work through your issues by writing in a journal or diary; writing poetry or music.
- Ask friends and others how they have let go of old baggage.

A woman at peace has stopped looking for someone to blame.

—Barbara Jenkins, author

Personalities Aren't Set in Concrete — Change Is Possible!

I WAS HAVING LUNCH WITH MY FRIEND Anita Goldstein one day and complaining to her about my frustration with my current boyfriend and my general difficulties in relationships with men.

"I'm very insecure.... I need a lot of attention and reassurance," I said.

"Up until now," Anita interrupted.

"Huh? What?" I asked, surprised.

"Up until now," she repeated. "Every time you hear yourself making some blanket statement like that, I'd suggest that you add those three words, 'up until now.' Every time you do that, you're making a break with the past. You're giving yourself permission to change. Just because you were a certain way in the past, does not mean that you necessarily have to be that way today ... or in the future. 'Up until now' acknowledges what was true in the past, but it also gives you freedom for something different in the future."

"Okay," I replied. "Up until now I have been insecure and needed a lot of attention."

"How does it feel when you say that?" she asked me.

"Different ... and awkward," I said. "Now I'm not sure how I feel about needing attention."

"Great!" she said. "Just be with that. Consider the possibility that maybe you've changed. Just because you were a certain way in the past, doesn't mean that you're still that way."

"Okay," I agreed.

"And remember that phrase, 'up until now,' and use it anytime you hear yourself making some kind of absolute judgment or statement about yourself. See if it makes a difference," she concluded.

That conversation occurred some twenty years ago, and it has made a huge difference in my life. It has given me freedom from the tyranny of the past and opened up new possibilities for change. When I catch myself making pronouncements about myself, especially negative pronouncements – "I'm disorganized," "I'm easily distracted," "I don't have a good memory for names," "I'm impulsive" – I correct myself mid-sentence with "Up until now I've been disorganized." In doing so, I give myself the freedom to change.

Language is powerful. My friend Anita taught me that three little words can transform my present and my future. I can give myself freedom by keeping the past in the past, and not letting the past dictate my future. So now, instead of saying, "I never write *New York Times* bestsellers," ... I can say, "Up until now, I haven't written a *New York Times* bestseller." Who knows? Maybe now I have!

Unless the knowledge gained from experience is reconditioned in each new situation, it is a rigid and a dangerous guide.

—Blanche H. Dow

It is never too late to be what you might have been.

—George Eliot (Mary Ann Evans), British writer

By the time your life is finished,
you will have learned just enough to begin it well.

—Eleanor Marx, author, youngest daughter
of Karl Marx

5

My Body/My Self

You can take no credit for beauty at sixteen.
But if you are beautiful at sixty, it will
be your soul's own doing.

—*Marie Carmichael Stopes, Scottish writer*

Women's bodies are both beautiful and practical. Our soft curves and alluring femininity have, for centuries, inspired the world's greatest artists. On the other hand, our innate physical durability enables us to give birth to babies and feed them, work hard, juggle multiple roles, and go the distance, outliving men. Our bodies are nothing short of miraculous – the epitome of "form follows function." Mother Nature knew what she was doing when she created the female body.

Some of us are not so thrilled with Mother Nature's handiwork. In fact, I don't know a single woman who actually likes her body. I'm sure there must be some who do, I just don't know any. Women worry and fret about being too fat, too tall, too short, too something! We worry about our health – menopause, cancer, heart disease, osteoporosis, chronic fatigue syndrome, arthritis, and other physical concerns. We worry about aging – the loss of physical beauty as well as the prospect of being old ladies in a society that worships youth.

Having a woman's body is definitely a mixed blessing. It gives me great pleasure and it gives me such a headache, too. I can tell you this for sure: My body is so high maintenance that if it were a car, I wouldn't buy it!

Wash Your Face — You'll Feel Better!

WHEN I WAS A LITTLE GIRL, occasionally I would get sick. Nothing serious, just the usual childhood stuff like measles, mumps, chicken pox, colds, and the croup. (I am not quite sure what the croup is, or if anybody still gets it anymore — I don't hear people talk about it.) When I got the croup, with lots of congestion in my chest, my mother would transform my bunk-bed into a tent — draping blankets from the top bunk to form a dark enclosure for me in the bottom bunk. Then she would place a vaporizer in the tent, turning it into a sweat lodge.

No matter what illness I had — nasty croup or simple cold — my mother would always say the same thing: "Wash your face — you'll feel better. When you look better, you'll feel a bit better, too." Sometimes I did as she suggested, sometimes not. What I found was that she was right. When I washed my face, I did feel better.

This sounds like such a simple lesson, but I can't tell you how many times it has helped me — not just in times of illness, but in times of fatigue, depression, sadness, or stress. If I am feeling bad and I remember to take a few minutes to wash my face, it perks me up. I feel refreshed, renewed, with just a wee bit more positive energy than before.

If I want to go a step further, I'll brush my hair and/or put on some fresh lipstick, and voilà! I feel significantly better. There's something about making myself more presentable, even if no one is around but me, that makes a difference in how I feel.

Health: what my friends are always drinking to before they fall down.

—Phyllis Diller, comedienne

The secret of staying young is to live honestly, eat slowly, and lie about your age.

—Lucille Ball, comedienne

Being pretty on the inside means you don't hit your brother and you eat all your peas — that's what my Grandma taught me.

—Elizabeth Heller, author of *Grandparents Are for Hugging*

Comfort Food

Sometimes I call my mother when I am sick. She answers the phone, "Hello?"

I bleat like a pathetic little goat, "I want my Mommy!"

She laughs. "What's the matter? Are you sick?"

Of course I'm sick! Do I sound like this when I'm well?

I know she can't come take care of me – she lives more than 100 miles away and has her own busy life. But I make the call anyway, just to make myself feel a little better, and to let her know that even today, as old as I am, when I feel lousy, I want the comfort that Mom used to bring me when I was little.

When I was sick as a child, she made milk toast for me. It was the perfect comfort food – warm, soft, mild, soothing. (Warm milk raises the seratonin level in the brain, which is why people drink it when they can't sleep – it induces a sense of well-being, and you drift right off into slumber.) It's simple, inexpensive, and easy to make – I usually have the ingredients to make it already in the house.

So, when I finish whining to Mom on the phone, I tell her goodbye, get out of bed, and go make myself some milk toast.

Mom's Milk Toast

Ingredients
   1-2 pieces of white bread toasted
   1 cup milk

continued

1 pat of butter

Salt to taste

Directions

Toast slices of bread.

Tear the toast into pieces and put it into a bowl.

Heat milk in the microwave or in a saucepan.

Pour heated milk over the toast.

Add a pat of butter and stir it around to help it melt.

Salt to taste.

Then take two aspirin, go back to bed, and call Mom again in the morning!

Physical Gratitude

I WENT TO VISIT MY FRIEND JO LAST WEEK. She had tumbled down some stairs a few days earlier, dislocating her right shoulder and fracturing her right arm. She was wearing a sling contraption that essentially strapped her arm to her body, keeping the injured limb immobilized and using her body as a splint. Fortunately, she didn't have to have surgery to repair the damage – she was lucky. But her right arm was going to be out of commission for weeks, and it would take her months of physical therapy to rebuild her strength and recover her mobility.

"How did you do this to yourself?" I asked her.

"Well, I wish I had some exciting story to tell you," she said, "but I was just vacuuming – standing at the top of the stairs with the vacuum wand in my hand, stretching to reach some cobwebs on the ceiling of the stairwell. I stretched too far, lost my footing, and down I went! Tumbling down the stairs is all a blur, but when I landed at the bottom of the stairs, my arm was hanging off the front of me, not the side. I was in such pain, I didn't know if I was gonna pass out or throw up."

"Eeew! Gross!" I said. "Okay, okay, enough with the gory details!"

We both laughed.

"I always knew that cleaning house was hazardous to your health," I joked. "You have given me proof!"

I brought Jo the things she had asked me to get for her at the store — an electric toothbrush and an electric can opener. "It's amazing all the things you suddenly can't do when your right arm is immobilized," she said. "I'm right-handed, and I can't brush my teeth; I can't open a can of cat food; I can't drive my car because is it a stick shift; I can't write checks or sign my name; and I can't use my computer! I feel so helpless!"

Jo is fortunate that she has lots of friends to help her out — people to bring her groceries, people to run errands, neighbors to come over and clean out the cats' litter box, and family to help as well. Her dad swapped cars with her so she could drive his automatic with her left hand and not have to shift gears. Jo is lucky to have a good support system and also lucky that she would recover from her injuries — they aren't permanent disabilities.

Jo's experience reminds me how fortunate I am to have a healthy body, with two arms and hands that work just fine, a strong back, and legs and feet that get me where I need to go. My eyes can see, my ears can hear, my senses are all fully operational. Aren't I lucky? I try to remember to be aware of my physical body and how well it serves me. I can bend and stoop, and stretch and reach as I go about my daily routine. It's the simple, daily activities that I take for granted — it's so easy to forget about my body — until it doesn't work, that is.

Visiting Jo reminds me how good I have it. Her experience tells me that I must be careful with my own body, to be aware when it is in danger — going down stairs, stepping off curbs, crossing streets, lifting heavy things, reaching for something in the back seat of the car, climbing ladders.

When I go for my morning walk I say a little prayer of thanks for the ability to walk. I thank my body for all its good work, and I thank the Divine for giving me this body. I am truly grateful.

I don't think jogging is healthy, especially morning jogging. If morning joggers knew how tempting they looked to morning motorists, they would stay home and do sit-ups.

—Rita Rudner, comedienne

Real Bodies

- The average American woman weighs 144 pounds and wears between a size 12 and a size 14.
- Marilyn Monroe wore a size 14.
- A psychological study in 1995 found that three minutes spent looking at a fashion magazine caused 70 percent of women to feel depressed, guilty, and shameful.
- Models twenty years ago weighed 8 percent less than the average woman. Today they weigh 23 percent less.
- There are 3 billion women who don't look like supermodels and only eight who do.

My Body Carma

I love cars. Maybe because I live in Los Angeles, car heaven . . . maybe because cars give me freedom and independence . . . maybe just because they're fun.

The cars we drive say a lot about who we are and what we value — safety, reliability, value for the dollar, sex appeal, speed and power, and individuality. Each type of car has its own personality. Knowing the kind of car a woman drives gives you some hints about who she is, or aspires to be.

If my body were a car . . . what kind of car would I be? Hmm . . . When I was a young woman, my body was like a Mazda Miata — slim, sporty, peppy, perky, cute, and ever-so-California in its styling. It was youthful and sexy in a wholesome kind of way. Unfortunately, I didn't take such good care of my Miata — I put inferior fuel into it; I didn't get it tuned up often enough; I didn't put it through its paces regularly in order to keep it in top condition; I was sometimes reckless in operating my car, so it got some dings and dents in it. It slowed down. It doesn't respond as quickly now as it did twenty years ago.

Today, my body is more like a Honda Accord — not a new one, a used one. It's not a bad car at all. In fact, it's pretty good. It's reliable and sturdy, although it is out of warranty and occasionally I have to do some major work on it. It's an attractive car, pleasant to look at and drive, but not a head-turner anymore. My Honda body is pretty responsive, starts up consistently in the morning, and gets me where I need to go. I try to take better care of it than I did my Miata, because I think I'd still have my Miata if I'd maintained it better. I don't want to lose my Honda as well as my Miata! Who knows what kind of car I would become next? An Edsel?

My *fantasy* body/car, of course, is different than my *actual* one. I'd love to be a sleek, sexy Jaguar XKE – long and lean, with a powerful engine that purrs quietly, ready to leap into action at a touch of the accelerator. In my dreams I am beautiful, classy, elegant, and high-powered as well as high-maintenance. I need a lot of attention and tending. I am not a car to be ignored or taken for granted.

Then I awake from my fantasy and here I am, back in my Honda. Could be worse, could be better. But . . . since the Honda Accord is the bestselling car in America, I guess I have nothing to complain about. All those people can't be wrong.

What kind of a car are *you*? A sports car, a sedan, a domestic car, an import, a truck, a minivan, a Beetle, a Benz? What are your best selling points?

Turning Boring,
Healthy Things into Games

MY COUSIN MARILYN JENSEN has this weird game she plays with fat. "I'm glad you like the lasagna I made," she says over dinner one evening, "There are only 3 grams of fat per serving. Isn't that great?!" She's so happy and proud of herself. She makes these pronouncements regularly when I have dinner at her house.

Marilyn is in her sixties and has some kind of heart problem for which she takes medication. Her boyfriend, who is in his seventies (Do we still call them boyfriends at that age?), has had a heart attack and bypass surgery. They both need to be diligent about eating a very low-fat diet.

"What a drag," I think to myself. "No Haägen-Dasz, no croissants at Starbucks, no burgers, no tacos, no eggnog, no butter cream frosting on cake, no Dove bars. Sheesh! What's the point in living?"

Marilyn sees it differently. She turned the task of counting grams of fat into a game for herself. Explaining it to me one evening she said, "I take regular recipes and substitute low-fat ingredients for the high-fat ones, and make it a personal challenge to see how low I can get the fat gram count. I make it into a contest for myself, a game. When I can get the fat gram count really low, then I win!" She grinned delightedly.

She loves to cook and clips recipes from the newspaper, collects cookbooks, and spends a lot of time in the kitchen preparing meals for her boyfriend and herself. They entertain friends and neighbors (and me!) often. The meals are always delicious, and I am always amazed.

Now, I'm not as excited about fat grams as my cousin Marilyn, but I realized that this is a great philosophy for dealing with other difficult tasks or projects – just turn them into games!

For instance, some authors hate asking important people for book endorsements – but, following Marilyn's example, I make it into a game, sort of like a scavenger hunt. The more endorsements I can collect for my newest book, the more I feel like I'm winning the game. I do the same thing with my income taxes – the more of my own money I can get back from the IRS each year, the higher my "score" – and I feel like I'm winning at the tax game.

Now, if only I can figure out how to turn getting a pelvic exam or a mammogram into a game!

Cousin Marilyn's Sunshine Salad

Ingredients
  1 bag (or 1 head) of romaine lettuce (you can also use
     baby spinach or red leaf lettuce)
  1 Bermuda onion
  1 can of mandarin orange slices
  1 lb. of peeled cooked shrimp (medium size)
  Trader Joe's Cranberry Trail Mix*   *continued*

 * If you don't have a Trader Joe's near you, find or make a trail mix
   that has dried cranberries, golden raisins, raw whole almonds, raw
   cashew pieces, raw pepitas, and sunflower seeds.

Low-fat raspberry vinaigrette dressing

Poppyseed dressing

Directions

Put lettuce in the salad bowl.

Open can of mandarin oranges and drain the juice off; add orange segments to lettuce.

Add shrimp to lettuce.

Chop up a Bermuda onion, add as much or as little as you like to the salad.

Cover and chill salad until ready to serve.

Just before serving salad, add cranberry trail mix to the salad.

Mix some poppyseed dressing with a little raspberry vinaigrette, usually 3 parts poppyseed to 1 part vinaigrette, and add to salad to taste – toss it, taste it, and see if needs a little more of any of the ingredients – add them to taste.

Serve! *A votre santé!*

Food is an important part of a balanced diet.

—Fran Lebowitz, writer, humorist

I really don't think I need buns of steel. I'd be happy with buns of cinnamon.

—Ellen DeGeneres, comedienne

Women Educating Other Women about Our Bodies

I TUNED IN TO WATCH *OPRAH* the other day, because I heard that she was doing a show on women and heart disease. I normally don't watch daytime TV, but I made it a point to watch, even taping a note to the fridge so I wouldn't forget. It was well worth my time. She had two physician guests – a female cardiologist and a male heart surgeon, both of whom had recently written books on heart health.

I learned that 1 out of 2 women in America today will die of heart disease, and that more women than men die of heart disease every year. I learned that heart disease is the number one killer of women over age thirty-five, and that 500,000 women die of heart disease every year (as compared to 40,000 who die from breast cancer). And I learned that only 6 percent of women today know the staggering odds stacked against their hearts being healthy.

I learned that, for a variety of reasons, black women are 69 percent more likely to die from heart attacks than white women. And I learned that 79 percent of black women in their sixties have heart disease.

Finally, I learned that there are simple, effective things that women can do to change their odds of getting (and dying from) heart disease. For instance, walking just ten blocks a day, every day, can reduce your chances of heart attack by 30 percent – and walking further, thirty minutes a day, can reduce your chances of heart attack by 50 percent!

I learned a lot of practical, helpful health facts from watching Oprah's show that day. I also learned something else – the power of women teaching other women about our bodies.

We have been sharing information with one another for thousands of years – mothers and grandmothers taught younger generations about menstruation, sex, pregnancy, and other important female health issues. Women friends have always shared with one another what they learned from their own experiences and illnesses. Today, living in the Information Age, we have more than oral traditions to pass on to one another – we have books, tapes, health magazines, medical journals, and of course, the Internet.

There are only a few women like Oprah who have talk shows and are in a position to educate and enlighten not just her own girlfriends, but millions of other women (Fact: 7 million viewers tune in to *Oprah!* each day). And women who watch *Oprah!* tell their friends, mothers, sisters, and others. It's mind-boggling the number of women Oprah reaches with her programs on women's health. Bless her.

The rest of us may not have the ability to inform and enlighten as many women as Oprah does, but we do have the opportunity to share health information with the dozens of women we know and love. Armed with the latest facts we glean from the Internet, from doctors, books, journals … and *Oprah!* … we can take charge of our own health and teach other women as well.

After watching Oprah's program on heart health, a new icon popped into my imagination – it was Saint Oprah, Our Lady of Perpetual Information, preaching a gospel of empowered women, personal responsibility, healthy self-care, positive relationships, and nurturing families. I think I'll put some flowers on the TV and offer her a quick prayer of thanks.

It's a fact

Leading Causes of Death among Women

Cause	White Women's Death Rate		Black Women's Death Rate	
	1970	1996	1970	1996
Heart disease	167.8	92.9	251.7	153.4
Cancers	107.6	107.6	123.5	130.7
Cerebrovascular diseases (i.e., strokes)	56.2	22.9	107.9	39.2
Unintentional injuries (accidents)	27.2	17.6	35.3	20.5
Pneumonia and influenza	15.0	10.1	29.2	12.9
Diabetes mellitus	12.8	10.7	30.9	29.4
Liver disease and cirrhosis	8.7	4.4	17.8	5.7
Suicide	7.2	4.4	2.9	2.0
Chronic obstructive pulmonary disease	5.3	18.3	N/A	13.1
Kidney diseases	N/A	3.1	N/A	8.5
HIV/AIDS	N/A	1.8	N/A	20.2

Deaths per 100,000 resident population; rates are age adjusted.
N/A = Data Not Available
Source: National Center for Health Statistics, 1998

Over the Hill . . . and the View Is Great!

I recall reading a story about Gloria Steinem, interviewed by a reporter on the occasion of her fiftieth birthday.

"You look great for your age," the young whippersnapper said to the living legend.

"I don't know what you mean," Steinem replied as she fixed him in her steady gaze.

"Well, I just mean, uh, . . . that you look good for someone who just turned fifty," he stammered.

"I still don't understand you . . . ," she said matter-of-factly. "This is what fifty looks like."

Everything you see I owe to spaghetti.

—Sophia Loren, actress

Even with all my wrinkles! I am beautiful!

—Bessie Delaney, 103-year-old author (with her sister Sadie) of *Having Our Say: The Delaney Sisters' First 100 Years*

Enjoy What We Have While We Have It

WOMEN DON'T TALK ABOUT THEIR BREASTS. At least, most of the women in my life don't talk about their breasts. It seems curious to me, since breasts seem so important to how we think of ourselves as women. (Our breasts certainly seem to be important to the men in our lives!) I recently asked my friend Jeannie about this odd silence about breasts. We were having one of those leisurely lunches on a warm spring afternoon, sipping iced tea and grazing on our favorite salads.

"I can't remember what my breasts looked like without stretch marks," Jeannie said. "I got pregnant when I was eighteen and had my baby when I was barely nineteen. I wish I had waited a while.... I would like to have enjoyed my perky little breasts while I still had them.

"I remember when the stretch marks showed up. Bright red they were, like two sunbursts on my chest. I was about halfway through my pregnancy. I freaked out! 'Isn't there something I can take to make the milk dry up?' I pleaded with the doctor. 'I don't need to breastfeed. Bottles will be fine.'

"'Nope,' he replied. 'Anything we could give you to dry up your milk would hurt the baby.'

The Five Stages of a Woman's Life

1 To Grow Up
2 To Fill Out
3 To Slim Down
4 To Hold It In
5 To Hell with It

"'What about rubbing cocoa butter on them? I heard that's good for preventing stretch marks,' I asked.

"He just laughed. 'Well, it'll give your husband something to do. But it won't make any difference with the stretch marks. The skin on your body is somewhat elastic – expanding and contracting as you gain weight with pregnancy and lose weight afterward. But some parts of the skin are more elastic than others. Like your tummy – see? You have no stretch marks there. But the skin on your breasts isn't as stretchy, and so you get those marks. Don't worry. Over time, they'll turn the same color as the rest of your skin and you'll hardly notice them.'

"'Easy for him to say,' I grumbled to myself. 'He's not the one walking around with two sunbursts on his chest. How come nobody ever warned me about this stuff? This pregnancy business is a drag – morning sickness that lasts well beyond morning, stretch marks, fatigue, swollen feet, raging hormones, and volatile emotions. If I'd known all this, I'd have made my husband use a condom!'"

"So, how did it turn out with the stretch marks?" I asked her.

"Well, of course, the doctor was right," she said. "The cocoa butter didn't do anything but make me feel like a big, fat, greasy chocolate bar. The baby arrived a few months later, and I was glad that I nursed him, even though his little gums were as hard as rock and my poor nipples were tender and chapped for the first few weeks of nursing. The stretch marks faded to the color of the rest of my skin, but I can still see them. And my breasts droop a bit –

'the headlights don't point straight ahead anymore,' as one of my friends says. I just wish I had enjoyed those perky little 34B breasts more while I still had them. I can't even remember what they looked like."

We laughed, realizing how easy it is for us to take our physical attributes for granted – to not even know how wonderful our features are until we lose them in the aging process. Whether it's our perky breasts, our firm buttocks, our slender waists, our hair color, our youthful, flexible joints, the strength and tone of our young muscles, the acuity of our senses, or our bodies' energy – we often don't notice how good something is until it's gone.

Jeannie and I had a bittersweet conversation that day over lunch, reminiscing about the bodies we had as young women. We decided that the old adage, "If you don't use it, you lose it," should have a new companion: "Better love it, 'cause later you'll lose it."

If I hadn't had them, I would have had some made.

—Dolly Parton, singer/songwriter, actress

It's impossible to be more flat-chested than I am.

—Candace Bergen, actress

I have everything I had twenty years ago, only it's all a little bit lower.

—Gypsy Rose Lee, stripper

A lot of guys think the larger a woman's breasts are, the less intelligent she is. I don't think it works like that. I think it's the opposite. I think the larger a woman's breasts are, the less intelligent the men become.

—Anita Wise, comedienne

Subject: BREASTS

(o)(o)	Perfect breasts
(+)(+)	Fake silicone breasts
(*)(*)	High nipple breasts
(@)(@)	Big nipple breasts
oo	A cups
{ O }{ O }	D cups
(oYo)	Wonder Bra breasts
(^)(^)	Cold breasts
(Q)(O)	Pierced breasts
(p)(p)	Hanging tassels breasts
\o/\o/	Grandma's breasts
(-)(-)	Flat against the shower door breasts
|o||o|	Android breasts
($)($)	Pamela Anderson's breasts

People say you shouldn't have plastic surgery because if God wanted you another way he would have made you that way, but I say that's a lot of crock. If God didn't want plastic surgeons, he wouldn't have given them hands to work with.

—Dolly Parton, singer/songwriter, actress

I'm the poster child. Any time there is an article on plastic surgery, my name will appear. Having plastic surgery is not shoplifting. People have treated it like, "Oh my God! She got plastic surgery!"

. . . Am I worried about it affecting my credibility? The doctor didn't remove my education and experience. . . . If I keep it quiet, hide, and lie, my credibility is supposed to be better?

—Greta Van Susteren, Fox news anchor (discussing her eye job)

Beauty can't amuse you, but brainwork — reading, writing, thinking — can.

—Helen Gurley Brown, former editor of *Cosmo* magazine

There is no cosmetic for beauty like happiness.

—Marguerite Gardiner Blessington, Irish writer

What Is BEAUTY?

Boundless
Energy
Acting
Uniquely
Tantalizingly
Yourself

6

Men and Marriage

Love is much nicer to be in than an
automobile accident,
a tight girdle, a higher tax bracket,
or a holding pattern over Philadelphia.

—Judith Viorst, writer

Men – now there's a topic that'll generate intense discussion in any group of women! What do you love about men? What drives you crazy about men? "Profound ambivalence" is probably an accurate way of summing up how many women feel about men. We spend years primping and grooming, competing with each other for the attention of men, but then we complain that we don't like the kind of attention we're getting. We want to be considered equal partners with men, but end up resenting that we seem to be doing more than our share of the work. We want men who are strong and confident, but then accuse them of being too controlling or domineering.

And *marriage* – there's another word that conjures up a wide variety of images. Some think of a white picket fence, 2.2 kids playing in the yard with the family dog. Others think of some romantic movie with deeply devoted soul mates in love for years and years on end. Still others recall their parents' less-than-perfect marriages and shudder, "If marriage is like that, I don't want any part of it!" But then how to be comfortably single in a world that still seems largely coupled up?

Oh, what shall we do about men and marriage? As an old proverb states, "You'll repent if you marry, and repent if you don't."

The Measure of a Man

WHAT THINGS DO WE WOMEN complain about concerning men? No shortage of answers to that question! They don't listen; they don't ask for directions; they're sloppy; they're self-absorbed; they snore; they're too interested in sex; they never talk about their feelings; they forget birthdays and other important dates; and the list goes on . . . okay, we have lots of complaints about men.

The question behind the question is this: What is the yardstick we use to evaluate men? What is our point of reference? To whom are we comparing men, and why do men always come up lacking?

The answer has the potential to profoundly change the way we look at men. We compare men to ourselves . . . to women. Compared to women, men have all these faults. We don't just compare men to women, though, we compare men to an idealized woman! Not an ordinary woman, but a woman at her best. Then men really come up deficient!

I was stunned when I learned this in a seminar called "Celebrating Men, Satisfying Women," taught by Alison Armstrong, who has been studying men for more than a decade. I went to her seminar because I, like lots of women, found men to be troublesome and difficult to understand, and my romantic relationships were disappointing and frustrating. I wanted to have good relationships with men — men at work, men in my family, men I was interested in romantically, and men in general.

What I learned from Alison is that I was using the wrong

yardstick to evaluate men. Comparing a man to an idealized woman and then condemning him for coming up short is like comparing a dog to a cat and criticizing the dog for not measuring up. A dog isn't supposed to be like a cat. A man isn't supposed to be like a woman. If I use the idealized woman as my yardstick, the man can't ever come out looking good — he ends up being judged as a defective woman!

This simple revelation has transformed my relationships with men. I changed yardsticks, and it has made all the difference. I learned from Alison that men are a different species from women. Just as cats and dogs are both four-footed mammals but are very different from one another — so, too, are men and women both two-footed humans, but very different from one another. When I see men for who they really are, they are wonderful beings! Many of the things I used to criticize men for, I now find just fine — sometimes even endearing!

I've learned to accept men the way they are and work with that. I made myself a whole lot happier in the process, and it makes the men in my life happier too!

Having a healthy relationship with a man means loving him for who he is now, and not loving him in spite of who he is today, or in hopes of who he will be tomorrow.
—Barbara DeAngelis, author, relationship expert

The Differences Are Hardwired

MEN ARE SINGLE-FOCUSED, while women are good at multi-tasking. Most of us know this, but it still frustrates us. Why can't men do more than one thing at a time? Why can't they listen to us and watch TV simultaneously? Why does it seem so easy for a woman to cook a meal, help the kids with their homework, throw a load of laundry into the dryer, and listen to the evening news all at the same time?

Have you noticed how differently we shop? Most men know exactly what they need when they go into a store – they make a beeline for that item, make their selection, and head to the cashier to pay for it. Women often know what they need, too – but they still take time to cruise the aisles, just in case they forgot to put something on their list, in case something good is on sale, or just to see what else is available. In short, men hunt and women gather.

I learned all this from Jennifer James, a well-known author and anthropologist who spoke at a professional conference I attended a few years ago. Dr. James has conducted extensive research on both primitive and advanced societies, analyzing historical trends and drawing lessons to help us understand ourselves and the world we live in today. Her research has led her into some fascinating areas – gender differences, racial diversity, tribes and clans, evolution of societies, changes in technology – and toward some implications for the future. I found her thoughts on male/female differences particularly helpful.

For many years I thought, along with many feminists, that boys and girls were more similar than different, but that their socialization led them to develop along different paths, resulting in significant differences between men and women.

According to Dr. James, many of these differences aren't learned, they're innate – they're hardwired. Men are single-focused because thousands of years ago their job was hunting – their mantra was "Hunt for game, hunt for game, hunt for game." They had to stay focused to succeed. When they killed an animal, they brought it back to the cave, and then they could turn their attention to the next task, eating. After that, sex. After that, sleep. So it went, a single focus on one activity at a time.

Women's work in those early eons was different. Their job was to gather berries, roots, and other edibles, while keeping one eye out for danger and another eye on the children. Their vision was always roving, scanning the environment for food and danger. The biological fact of their smaller size, plus their sole ability in child-bearing and lactation meant that women could not take on the male role of hunting. In short, biology was destiny.

Today, my son can't seem to hear me when he's watching TV; my brother doesn't want to carry on a conversation while he's cooking dinner; my father won't answer the phone if there's a football game on. Is there something wrong with them? No, they're just single-focused. When they're focused on me, it's lovely. Then I have their full attention. If they're focused on something else, I might as well give it up and wait for them to finish what they're doing.

In the meantime, I think I'll go to my study, pay some bills, listen to NPR, wrap a birthday gift for a friend, and talk to my best friend on the phone. What, oh what, shall I do with all the energy I have left over?

The test of man is how well he is able to feel about what he thinks.

The test of a woman is how well she is able to think about what she feels.

—Mary McDowell

The woman's vision is deep reaching — the man's far reaching.

With the man, the world is his heart; with the woman, the heart is her world.

—Betty Grable, actress

Genderspeak: He Said, She Said

MY COLORFUL FRIEND CAROLE taught me about the importance of discerning what men are really saying rather than what you *think* they are saying. She tells "Tom stories" to illustrate her point (Tom is her husband, a charming all-American kind of guy). Carole and Tom like to buy fixer-upper houses, spending months, especially on weekends, getting the place in shape.

On a typical Saturday morning, Carole will be in one room, and Tom shouts from another room, "Carole, where's the tape measure?"

"I think it's in the toolbox," Carole replies.

Silence.

"Carole, where's the tape measure?" Tom asks again, this time exasperated.

The light bulb goes off in Carole's head. "He's not asking me where the tape measure is," she thinks to herself. "What he's really saying is, 'Carole, bring me the tape measure.'"

A similar conversation sometimes takes place in the early evening, when they both get home from work. "Is there anything to eat in the house?" Tom asks.

Unthinking, Carole replies, "Yes, there is."

Silence.

"What is there to eat in the house?" Tom rephrases his question.

Foolishly, Carole starts to list what she recalls from the fridge: "There are quite a few things – steak left from the barbecue we had the other night, the makings for spaghetti, sandwich stuff, salad stuff, some nice salmon I bought at the store yesterday, fruit. . . ."

She looks up to see Tom frowning, and suddenly realizes that the real question is, "What are you going to make us to eat?"

Sometimes I marvel how anyone stays coupled up with their spouse given how different we are from men! I can only surmise that the advice Carole gave me must be true. For a happy, successful marriage, she says: The woman should love her man a little, and understand him a lot; and the man should love his woman a lot, and understand her not at all!

Given the cultural barriers to inter-sex conversation, the amazing thing is that we would even expect women and men to have anything to say to each other for more than ten minutes at a stretch. The barriers are ancient — perhaps rooted, as some paleontologist may soon discover, in the contrast between the occasional guttural utterances exchanged in male hunting bands and the extended discussions characteristic of female food-gathering groups.

—Barbara Ehrenreich, journalist

If love is the answer, could you please rephrase the question?

—Lily Tomlin, comedienne, actor, author

Top Ten Things I've Learned about Men

1 Men are simpler than women. What you see is pretty much what you get.

2 Men are single-focused. Don't expect them to multi-task.

3 Men need to be right. They like to win.

4 Men are either attracted to you or they're not. Don't go to great lengths to try to win a man who isn't attracted to you. Watch for the ones who are.

5 Men like the chase.

6 Most men have a much higher sex drive than women. It's biological – their bodies and minds are hardwired for frequent sex. It doesn't make them bad or dirty – it just makes them men.

7 Men want sex and trade intimacy to get it. Women want intimacy and trade sex to get it.

8 Many of men's emotions get expressed as anger. They've been socialized not to express other emotions. Fear comes out as anger; frustration comes out as anger; sadness comes out as anger; even jealousy comes out as anger.

9 Men need women. Most of them don't do well without us. They get sick more often, they make less money, and they die sooner without a woman in their lives. Most men know this.

10 Men love and want women, but they often don't understand us. They love us because we're so different from them – complex, paradoxical, emotional, expressive, beautiful. But the differences also confuse them. They sometimes don't know how to make us happy.

Marrying a man is like buying something you've been admiring for a long time in a shop window. You may love it when you get it home, but it doesn't always go with everything in the house.

—Jean Kerr, playwright

You will never meet anyone without faults. If you marry, do so with someone whose faults you can live with. Some people's you can't.

—Edith Fripp, mother of speaker
and author Patricia Fripp

If you seek out a man in need of rehabilitation, you may well discover you're in for a bumpy ride.

—Sonya Friedman, author of *Men Are Just Desserts*

Attracting the Right Partner

WOMEN'S ADVICE ON FINDING a romantic partner seems to fall into two opposing schools of thought. One group of women tells me to focus, make it a goal, and keep a visual picture of my ideal partner in my consciousness at all times. Here's a sampling of their advice and experience:

"Once I decided I wanted to get married, finding the right guy happened fairly quickly," my friend Karyn said matter-of-factly at our monthly women's group meeting.

"I decided to treat the task of finding a husband like I would finding a job — I made it a project," my friend Judith explained to me on the phone one day.

"People who want to have relationships, have them. And people who don't, don't," Shakti Gawain pointed out in a seminar on "Creative Visualization."

"My feeling has always been that once a woman has the man she wants in her sights, he might as well accept it, because she's going to get what she wants," my dear friend Joan Hill has told me on more than once occasion.

Women in the opposite school of thought tell me to stop looking — love shows up when you least expect it.

"I was quite happy being single," Beverly told me. "I wasn't looking for a husband; I wasn't interested in getting married; my life was just fine the way it was. But then Danny showed up, swept me off my feet, and so now I'm married."

Patty's story is similar: "I'm in my early fifties, and at my age, I thought that finding a husband was out of the question. I was divorced and just figured I would spend the rest of my life single. You could have knocked me over with a feather when Paul, who had been a good friend from church, started asking me out on dates, and ultimately asked me to marry him. Never in my wildest dreams would I have imagined myself married again."

My friend Valerie described her experience. "I had decided I would never marry. I had several disappointing relationships with men, and had given up on them. I decided to devote my life to God and to my work. I was quite happy. Then Randy showed up in my life, and we ended up getting married.... My advice is: Quit looking for a man. Give it up. Just get on with your life and when you least expect it, someone might show up."

So, whose advice to take?

The power of intention is well documented in psychological research and many books. Olympic athletes visualize themselves vaulting hurdles, setting records, and winning gold medals. Entrepreneurs create wildly successful businesses, starting with nothing more than an idea they're passionate about. Their success started in their minds, with a decision to do something, with a goal to achieve, and with a clear picture in their consciousness of what it was they were after.

The power of serendipity is also well documented. Great discoveries are made by people who weren't looking for them at all. Chance meetings, mysterious coincidences, and surprise encounters often lead to amazing outcomes. Great treasure is sometimes found in the most unlikely places.

Which shall I do? Make a strategic plan and start my hunt for Mr. Right? Or, tear up my list of characteristics of my perfect partner, and leave it up to fate? Beats me. Maybe I'll just flip a coin.

A woman gets lonely, and sometimes she can't wait around for a man to be reincarnated.

—Agent Scully, *The X Files*

Men are my hobby; if I ever got married, I'd have to give it up.

—Mae West, actress

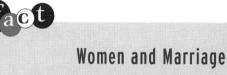

Women and Marriage

- In 1998, 58 percent of women eighteen years old and over were married, 21 percent had never married, and 11 percent each were widowed and divorced.

- The estimated median age at first marriage was twenty-five years for women in 1998, up almost a full five years since the early 1960s.

- The number of women living alone doubled between 1970 and 1998, from 7.3 million to 15.3 million, or 14 percent of all women fifteen years old and over. Half of the women living alone were elderly; put another way, 41 percent of all elderly women lived by themselves.

- All in all, 30.2 million households in 1998 – about 30 percent of the nation's total – were maintained by women with no husband present. In 1970, there were 13.4 million such households, comprising about 20 percent of all households.

(Source: U.S. Census Bureau)

Variety Is the Spouse...
Er, *Spice* of Life!

GWEN IS A BEAUTIFUL, elegant woman of eighty-six – still stunning after all these years. She has been married for fifty-five years to the same man, spending forty of those years in glamorous Aspen, ski resort of the rich and famous. Gwen has had many friends – a veritable Who's Who of literary, musical, and sports celebrities: comedian Steve Martin, singer John Denver, philosopher Mortimer Adler, musician Jascha Heifetz, ski champion Stein Erikson, and singer Andy Williams, to name just a handful.

Gwen is as wise as she is beautiful. She is intelligent and insightful – she doesn't suffer fools gladly. She is worldly and sophisticated and has seen human beings at both their best and their worst. She has the ability to reflect on her decades of life experience and to distill bits of wisdom to pass along to her daughter Danielle, and Danielle's friends, of whom I am one.

Since I have been single for many years, I often ask people who have been married a long time or who are in committed long-term relationships, "What's the secret of a long, happy relationship?" I've heard many answers in my years of asking the question:

- "You have to strike the right balance between time together and time apart."
- "Love is a great degree of tolerance."
- "The key to a long marriage is a short memory."

- "The ability to compromise and forgive is essential to a successful marriage."
- "Say 'Yes' to whatever he says, and then do what you want anyway."

And others ... some serious, some humorous, some ironic, some inspiring.

Gwen's answer to the question was truly original. She said, "The key to having a long, happy marriage is that you shouldn't depend on one man to satisfy all your needs."

"What do you mean?" I asked, intrigued by the implications of her comment. What was she going to tell me? Is she going to suggest that I develop more women friends ... or is there something more risqué in her statement?

"I think every woman should have three men in her life," Gwen said.

Ha! I thought to myself. A male harem – what a fabulous idea! I nodded my agreement.

"Yes, three men," Gwen smiled, " ... a gay guy to enjoy with arts with, a stud muffin for the bedroom, and an athlete to bring you adventure and activity."

Something was missing. "What about a husband?" I asked her.

"Oh, well, any one of those three could be your husband – you decide," she replied.

The woman is brilliant, I tell ya, brilliant!

There's just one thing ... I have a hard enough time finding one right guy – how on earth am I supposed to find *three*?!

There is so little difference between husbands,
you might as well keep the first.

—Adela Rogers St. Johns, journalist, screenwriter

Bigamy is having one husband too many.
Monogamy is the same.

—Erica Jong, author of *Fear of Flying*

Men Just Want to Make Us Happy

I WAS TALKING TO MY DAD on the phone not too long ago. "What are you up to these days?" I asked him.

"Just trying to stay out of trouble," he replied.

"Trouble? What gets you into trouble?" I queried.

"Everything," came his glum reply. "If I don't talk at dinner, I get in trouble. If I talk about the wrong thing at dinner, I get in trouble. If I talk too much, I get in trouble."

"Poor Daddy," I sighed gently. "Sounds like married life is hard."

"I just try to stay out of trouble," he muttered.

I got off the phone and was thinking about what my friend Alison Armstrong told me about marriage. "Our men really do want to make us happy. But if they can't make us happy, they'll settle for not making us upset." I could see living proof of this in my dad's relationship with my stepmother. He loves her dearly and he would do anything to make her happy. He just can't figure out what it is. Since he can't seem to make her happy, he settles for just trying not to make her upset.

Alison is a very wise women, and she has learned a lot about men, both in her single life and in her married life. She says, "Too many women want their men to be mind readers. 'If he loves me, he should know what I want!' we complain. Wrong! Men aren't mind readers. You can save yourself and your man a lot of headache by simply telling him what will make you happy. Don't make him guess, because if he guesses wrong too many times, he'll finally just give up. If he can't make you happy, he'll give up and settle for not making you upset."

Thanks to Alison, I've learned not to make men guess. Heaven knows, men find women mysterious enough as it is — I try not to make the guys more miserable by asking them to read my mind. . . Only other women can read my mind!

*Do let him read the papers. But not while you accusingly
tiptoe around the room, or perch much like a silent bird
of prey on the edge of your most uncomfortable chair.
(He will read them anyway, and he should read them, so
let him choose his own good time.) Don't make a big exit.
Just go. But kiss him quickly, before you go, otherwise he
might think you are angry; he is used to suspecting he is
doing something wrong.*

—Marlene Dietrich, actress

*Let your husband wear the pants in the family,
but be sure to lay his clothes out for him in the morning.*

—Betty Barr, Phyllis Barr's mom (Phyllis is a banker)

*Recently I listened as a broadcast interviewer asked a
group of teenagers what they would look for in a
mate.... Thinking of the evolutionary theories...I
waited for a modern variation on the male's allegedly
age-old desire for an attractive, fertile, narrow-
waisted woman and the female's preference for a
resource-rich, willing-to-commit man. Instead, girls
and boys all said the same thing: They want to marry
their soul mates. Don't we all?*

—Dianne Hales, author of *Just Like a Woman*

What Makes Men Happy?

SHANNON WAS FIGHTING BACK tears all through our monthly women's group meeting. Others asked if she was okay, and she nodded bravely. She was a pretty girl, in her twenties, and a little on the chubby side. Finally, the floodgates opened and the tears streamed down her face. "I'm so scared," she sobbed. "I'm getting married in three months, and I've been dieting, but I can't seem to lose weight."

"It's okay," we reassured her, like so many mother hens clucking around our young chick. "You are so pretty. Todd loves you just the way you are, or he wouldn't be marrying you. You've just got the pre-wedding jitters. You'll be fine."

Shannon was inconsolable. Her tears came in a torrent and her words came between sobs. "I've been reading this book on marriage and it says in there that there are three things that are most important to men in their marriage: sex, companionship, and having a woman who is attractive. I'm afraid that if I can't take off some weight, or worse yet, if I put on some weight, that he won't want me. I won't be able to make him happy!"

We hens kept clucking until our chick seemed calmer. We could all identify with her fear – fear of losing someone she loved very much, fear of being unattractive. What woman hasn't felt that, at least once in her life?

This was the first time I had heard of that formula about the three most important things to men in marriage. I decided to check it out with my younger brother, who is sort of your classic guy's guy – he's always been my source of information when I need someone who can speak for his gender.

I related what Shannon had told me she read in the book. "Is that true?" I asked my brother.

He didn't hesitate. "Yup, pretty much," he replied, "and they've got 'em in the right order too. When I think back on the ten years I've been married, and what makes me unhappy, it's one of those items. If my wife and I aren't having enough sex, I get unhappy. If she's working too many long days at work and I don't get to spend enough time with her, I get unhappy. The third thing – well, that's never a problem because my wife is always gorgeous."

"Anything else you wanna know?" he added.

"Nope," I replied. "You answered my question."

I haven't done a big survey to see if other men agree with my brother, and I never did get the name of that book from Shannon, but I think what they said is probably true. If any of you reading this book find out differently, will you let me know?

Women complain about sex more often than men. Their gripes fall into two major categories: (1) Not enough, and (2) Too much.

—Ann Landers, advice columnist

Bake Someone Happy

In the 1800s, Fanny Fern, an American writer, wrote, "The way to a man's heart is through his stomach" – words that women have repeated for generations. I believed them. I had watched my mother cater to Dad's sweet tooth for many years, so I simply followed suit when I got married. I made big breakfasts on weekends – either biscuits and gravy or homemade donuts (deep-fried in shortening and rolled in sugar). I baked sugar cookies the size of basketballs, chocolate cake cookies, oatmeal-Rice-Krispie-coconut cookies to die for, homemade fudge, and of course, cheesecake. I was a regular Betty Crocker – and my poor husband was turning into the Pillsbury Doughboy! He gained twenty pounds the first two months we were married! Poor guy – he would go to the gym and work out for an hour or two, then come home and eat a big slab of homemade cheesecake. And he wondered why he kept gaining weight. . .

What's your favorite love food?

Till-Death-Do-You-Part Cheesecake

Ingredients

16 double graham crackers
1½ cups sugar
¼ cup melted butter

6 three-ounce packages of cream cheese

4 eggs

Vanilla

3 cups sour cream

Directions

Crust

Crush the double graham crackers (put crackers between two sheets of wax paper and use a rolling pin to crush them, four or five crackers at a time).

Mix in ⅓ cup sugar and ¼ cup melted butter; mix well and press into a 9-inch square pan (or round pie pan).

Filling

Using electric mixer, mix together cream cheese, 1 cup sugar, eggs, and 2 tsp. vanilla; mix well and pour into crust.

Bake 30 minutes at 350 degrees F.

Topping

Mix together sour cream, 7 Tbsp. sugar, 3 tsp. vanilla.

Spoon gently over top of cheesecake and bake again for 25 minutes at 350 degrees F.

Let cool 1 hour and refrigerate 24 hours before serving.

Serve your sweetheart this and he'll love you till he dies . . . which will probably be when his arteries clog up with all the fat and cholesterol!

Men, Marriage, and Money

MY MOTHER AND FATHER DIVORCED after more than thirty years of marriage. Their marriage had actually started to go bad about fifteen years before, but it took a long time for it to slowly unravel. I asked my mother later, "Why didn't you leave years ago? Why did you hang in there so long, since you were so unhappy?"

"Where was I going to go?" she replied. "I had only one year of college, no work experience, no marketable skills that I could see, and I had two children. What could I do? I had to stay married."

Her unhappiness was a lesson to me: Later, when I found myself in an unhappy marriage, I left after only four years. I wasn't going to hang in there being miserable year after year. I had no idea where I was going to go, or what I would do to earn a living – and I had a three-year-old son. I knew one thing – I was young, healthy, smart, and resourceful – I would figure something out. I thought about my mother's years of quiet misery and vowed that I would never stay with a man for money. I would go out and earn my own money. If I found a man to share my life with, that would be gravy – we could share our money and our lives. I vowed not to let myself become trapped by a lifestyle or standard of living – or a lack of marketable skills.

I had read Germaine Greer when I was a teenager, but I didn't fully understand what she was writing about until my mother's and my own experiences brought the financial lesson home to me. Greer wrote that a woman must have her own money if she is to be truly her own person. She doesn't have control of her own life if she has to ask a man for money.

As a young girl, I had to ask my dad for money. I recall wanting a tape recorder when I was in junior high school – I had to plead and wheedle for months before he finally relented. Several years later, I needed a car when I went away to college – but it wasn't until he visited the college himself and saw the importance of wheels in Los Angeles that he gave me the old family car. He always controlled the purse strings, and he held them tightly.

When I got married, my husband took over Dad's role. I remember once having to explain to him why I bought artichokes out of season – they were expensive and he was upset with me. I hated asking him for money, and I hated having to justify my purchases.

My mother's experience showed me the pain of being trapped for lack of money and the fear of not being able to support oneself. Germaine Greer added weight and credibility to the notion of being self-supporting. Today I own my own home; I buy insurance; I pay my taxes; I go on trips; I buy clothes and jewelry; and I even have savings and a little invested. If Mr. Right ever does come along, yes indeed, he'll be gravy. But I won't want him for his money. . . I just hope he doesn't want me for mine!

Dear BJ,

Mostly, I have learned from my mother. This was more by example and circumstance than by any given instruction or discussion.

First, I learned that a woman must be self-sufficient. You cannot rely on a man, family, or others to support your life or your children's lives. You need to be independent. This means you should get work in a position that will bring you the income you need to support you and children (if you want them) — always.

Second, there are some things you have no control over. Therefore, I learned that you need to be flexible. Don't think that because you are married today that you will be married tomorrow. Tomorrow you may have a new job and a new husband or neither — be prepared to cope physically, financially, and emotionally.

Best always,
Cheri Toomey Uno
painter and potter

You can't put a price tag on love, but you can on all its accessories.

—Melanie Clark

Marriage is a bargain. And somebody has to get the worst of a bargain.

—Helen Rowland, author of *Reflections of a Bachelor Girl*

Before accepting a marriage proposal, take a good look at his father. If he's still handsome, witty, and has all his teeth . . . marry him instead.

—Diane Jordan

7

Women @ Work

The problem with the rat race is that,
even if you win, you're still a rat.

—Lily Tomlin, comedienne, author, actress

What is women's work? Some women see their work as building nests and raising the next generation. Some say their work is to make a difference and to build a better world. Some focus on putting food on the table and keeping the wolf from the door. Many of us say, "All of the above!"

We can learn much about work from other women, and much about ourselves from work — lessons of creativity and courage, lessons in dealing with adversity, lessons in conflict and collaboration, and lessons in leadership. So much to learn, so little time! Women's work has always been — and probably always will be — 24/7.

Working to Live or Living to Work?

"IF I COULD ASK YOU ONLY ONE QUESTION, what question should I ask to find out the most important things about you?" I asked my Life History class one day. "What question would lead me to the real essence of who you are?"

"Ask me about my art," one woman replied. "I am an artist, and my work is central to who I am. I don't exist without my art."

I was struck by her simple but powerful comment. It prompted me to think about the role of work in my own life. Is my identity wrapped up in being a writer and seminar leader? Or is that simply what I do to make a living?

For many years, I think my primary identity was being Michael's mom. Being a parent was such a huge job, and it consumed much of my time, energy, and attention. I felt that raising my son was the most important work I would ever do, and I wanted to do it well. The work that I did to earn money was simply a means to an end. I worked to live, not vice versa.

Over the years I've changed, and today I live to work. I have a mission, a purpose, something larger than myself, and it isn't wrapped around another person. I no longer think that being a parent is the most important work I will ever do. Contributing to people's lives through my books and seminars makes a much bigger impact on the world than raising my son. That's not to say that raising him well wasn't important — it definitely was . . . especially to him! But in terms of the sheer number of people that my life touches, and the difference I can make in the world, my work today is most important.

How do *you* decide what's more important and what's less important? I once read an interesting article about the mission statement that Mary Kay Ash developed for herself and the women who sell her cosmetics – it's essentially "God first; Family second; Career third." Sweet, simple, and succinct. It worked for her and for thousands of successful sales consultants who cruise around in their pink Cadillacs. Mary Kay's faith made her priorities easy to figure out.

For many women today, family comes first and everything else takes a back seat. For others, it is career first, with achievement and financial success at the top of their list. Remember: There are no right or wrong answers on this question – only choices.

That artist-student who spoke up in my class reminded me to check in with myself every so often, and ask, "Who am I? Why am I here? What is the meaning of my life?" and, "How is my identity evolving through different stages of life?"

What is the role of work in *your* life? Do you work to live? Are you like my student, and live to work? What's the most important question I should ask you – to find out who you really are?

Women's Work

All over the world, women's work is essentially cyclical and unending; the tasks are not the kind that lend themselves to closure. And it's not just child-raising. The difference goes back to the organization of hunter-gatherer societies. Men get together and go out for the occasional big kill, a specific event that has a climax, and then it's over.

But the women, who plant and gather, work at continuous tasks that need to be done again and again. This leads them to have more of a process orientation; and when you focus on process rather than achievement or closure, you get more satisfaction from the work itself.

You get pleasure from the actual doing of it, rather than from the abstract notion of getting it done.

–Diana Meehan, Director,
   Institute for the Study of Women and Men in Society at the
   University of Southern California

Raising the Bar

JANINE IS A HANDSOME WOMAN from Belize. Tall and elegant, she has a lovely British accent. She was the key staff person in the department I was hired to manage at a large corporation in downtown Los Angeles.

Janine had been with the company for more than twenty years. Starting off in the Human Resources Department as a new immigrant to this country, she had worked full-time, married, started a family, completed a bachelors degree at night, and was very active in Junior Achievement and Toastmasters. She had never risen above an hourly-wage position with the company, though, because people thought she was dumb.

Early in her career, someone had decided that Janine wasn't too bright, so she got shuffled around from one low-level clerical job to another — despite the fact that she had earned her BA, and was working on her masters degree when I became her boss. I'm not sure why people thought she was dumb — maybe because she spoke slowly and deliberately in that British way of hers, people surmised that she thought slowly as well.

She wasn't a top performer. She seemed mediocre at best to me. I complained to my boss. "I'm managing a very small department, and I really need Janine to perform at a higher level. Her job is critical to the whole department."

"Well, why don't you just get rid of her?" he asked.

"I can't do that — not without giving her a chance to improve," I replied.

"Whatever you want to do is fine with me," he shrugged. "But don't expect too much. She's not very bright, you know."

Later in the week I sat down with Janine to talk about her job. "I don't know how things were with your previous boss," I began, "but your level of performance is not cutting it with me. I'm gearing up to dramatically increase the productivity of this department, and your position has to play a central role in that."

She listened attentively.

"I'm willing to give you time to improve," I continued, "but I need you to be at this new level of performance within ninety days, or else I'm going to have to find someone else to do the job."

She said she understood.

After ninety days, we sat down to review her performance. Much to my surprise and delight, she was performing up to my level of expectation in almost every way!

What made the difference? Here's my take: Janine had been pigeonholed early in her tenure with the company, and because people decided she was dumb no one ever asked very much of her. Her bosses over the years expected mediocre performance and that's exactly what they got. In raising the bar, I gave Janine an opportunity to surprise everyone.

Since that day, Janine finished her master's degree, and went on to complete a Ph.D. I was able to redesign and reclassify her job so that she became a professional, no longer a clerical person. A few years ago she took early retirement and now has a second career as an education consultant.

Janine taught me the power expectations have to shape results. She reminded me that if you set high standards for yourself and others, you will most likely get high performance. If you set low goals, you'll get low performance.

Janine is a major success story. All I did was set the goal – she's the one who did the work to reach it. I'm honored to know her. I think of her whenever I am feeling lazy or considering accepting something as "good enough." As Debbie Fields, the cookie queen, famously said, "Good enough never is."

The goal must not be to find a job, but to become a magnificent woman.

—Marianne Williamson, author, spiritual teacher

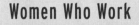

Women Who Work

- In 1950, one in three American women of working age had a paying job; today almost three in four do. At some point in their lives, 99 percent of women in the United States will work for pay.

- In two of every five American families, women are the sole earners; one in four makes more than her husband.

- The percentage of working married women who also have school-age children – now 77 percent – is expected to grow to an estimated 80 percent in the next decade.

- In the U.S., women fill 48 percent of corporate managerial and professional jobs, 43 percent of economists, 33 percent at a decision-making level in government, and 43 percent of enlisted soldiers.

- In other fields they still lag far behind: only 8 percent of engineers, 12 percent of military officers, 15 percent of architects, and 10 percent of apprentices in the trades are women.

(Source: *Just Like a Woman* by Dianne Hales)

Women Bosses and Bossy Women

OVER THE PAST TWENTY TO TWENTY-FIVE YEARS, I've had the opportunity to work for a number of women bosses:

There was Sharleen – the very epitome of evil. Manipulative, dishonest, but very, very smart, she ran her office like Stalinist Russia – keeping her staff at odds with one another by planting seeds of suspicion and doubt in each of our minds, instilling fear that others in the office had been complaining to her about us. She encouraged tattle-tales, back-stabbers, and gossips. I think secretly she was afraid that one day we would all get together and stage a coup – the princesses overthrowing the queen. So she instinctively kept us stirred up and divided. I'm not even sure she was doing it consciously – she was such an awful person that this was probably just her natural way of being.

Then there was Terry – as different from Sharleen as day is from night. Terry was bright and talented, and she was also kind, caring, thoughtful, gracious, compassionate, and a good listener. She genuinely cared about her staff, and it showed. She was firm and had a definite vision for where our organization was going. She had principles and integrity. Men and women alike respected her and trusted her. She was wonderful.

Finally there was Liz – different from both Terry and Sharleen. Liz was a good person – she had worked for many years with the Girl Scouts of America and had that nice Girl Scout kind of energy about her. She was perky and peppy, wholesome as apple pie and baseball, outgoing and friendly. She was a wonderful person, but a pretty lousy boss. She was disorganized and scattered. She was a problem solver, not a visionary – that is, she was okay at execution but no good at strategy. She rarely took the time to provide coaching or feedback to her staff, as she was always running off to meetings. She read her mail and took phone calls while I was trying to have individual meetings with her. She was indeed frustrating to work for!

What I learned from these women, and other bosses I've known, is that – surprise, surprise – women bosses aren't all that different from men bosses. Just as there are many kinds of male bosses – the good, the bad, and the downright ugly – there are many kinds of female bosses.

Some women have told me that they dislike working for women bosses – they perceive women with authority as demanding, picky, controlling, competitive, and even mean. Other women say that they prefer working for women bosses – they are good listeners, they're smart, they share information, they're supportive, and they're good team players. Who's right? I think Golda Meir, the former Prime Minister of Israel summed it up nicely: "Whether women are better than men I cannot say . . . but I can say they are certainly no worse."

I think of my boss as a father figure. That really irritates her.

—Mary Jo Crowley, journalist

Increasingly, motherhood is being recognized as an excellent school for managers, demanding many of the same skills: organization, pacing, the balancing of conflicting claims, teaching, guiding, leading, monitoring, handling disturbances, imparting information.

—Sally Helgeson, author of *The Female Advantage*

Some women have the attitude that they have fought to get to the top [so they're not about to give a helping hand to a woman on the rise]. It's shocking that we aren't mentoring other women, and that we are considering them our enemies.

—Mindy Morgenstern, author of *The Real Rules for Girls*

Women must understand that it's not another woman who is the enemy, but the power structure that sets it up for very few women to get jobs and make them fight each other for the few goodies that are thrown their way. We don't tend to see structural or institutional problems. We focus on the other person. We can't.

—Michelle Paludi, developmental psychologist, Hunter College, New York City

It's a fact

Education and Income

- In the U.S. today women receive 37 percent of MBAs, 43 percent of medical degrees, and 41 percent of law school diplomas.

- American women earn about three-quarters of what men do in comparable jobs. In certain areas, the income gap is narrowing – for instance, in science and technology entry-level positions, where college-educated women age 24 to 33 earn 98 percent of what their male counterparts do. However, as women advance, salary discrepancies remain entrenched.

(Source: *Just Like a Woman*, by Dianne Hales)

Walking the Corporate Tightrope

ANN MORRISON UNDERSTANDS THE DILEMMA that women face working in male environments. Her book, *Breaking the Glass Ceiling,* outlines our dilemma in excruciating detail. Traditionally, male behavior has been defined as decisive, take charge, in control, aggressive, competitive, and authoritative. Traditional female behavior has been defined as receptive, compliant, nurturing, caretaking, sensitive, cooperative, sharing, and submissive. There is just a little overlap between the two spheres that have been defined as masculine and feminine – qualities such as hardworking, honest, productive, and effective might fall into that overlapping of the two spheres.

As women who work in male environments, we must confine ourselves to that narrow band of behavior where the two circles overlap. If we act in a way that is seen as traditionally feminine, we are criticized as being too soft, too weak, and not tough enough to move up the corporate ladder. On the other hand, if we act in a way that is seen as traditionally masculine, then we are criticized as being too aggressive, too intense, and too competitive. Trying to be one of the boys inevitably backfires.

In short, there are two ways to fail and only one way to be successful. We must walk a fine line, a tightrope of acceptable behavior that is neither too feminine nor too masculine. If we can master that, we might, just might, have a chance of making it to the top. Ann Morrison helped me understand my own predicament working in a "good ol' boy" environment. I knew lots of other women in the company who were struggling with the same dilemma. How could we be successful in a large, bureaucratic organization that had been owned and run by men forever?

The answer to that question is a deeply personal one, and each woman has to answer it for herself. Some women stay in their jobs and quietly work to be successful so they can change the system from the inside out. Other women leave their companies in search of more women-friendly organizations. Still others do more than change companies – they change industries, looking for a place where the glass ceiling is not so thick. Some leave to start their own businesses. "If we can't be successful under the boys' rules," they say, "we'll just go out and start our own game!"

The fact that 75 percent of all new businesses in the past twenty years have been started by women tells us something: Many women are fed up trying to play a game they just can't win.

On a surface level for the majority of corporations, not discriminating against women is rewarded. You just don't hear certain kinds of things. We have come far. But the next mountain is harder to climb, and that is all the stuff you can't see, feel, or touch, but it's there. It's the subtle, subliminal discrimination.

—Brenda Snyder, President of U.S. West Women

How to Tell a Businessman from a Businesswoman

- A businessman is aggressive; a businesswoman is pushy.

- A businessman is good on details; she's picky.

- He loses his temper at times because he's so involved in his work; she's bitchy.

- He knows how to follow through; she doesn't know when to quit.

- He stands firm; she's hard.

- He is a man of the world; she's been around.

- He isn't afraid to say what he thinks; she's mouthy.

- He's a stern taskmaster; she's hard to work for.

  (Source: Marilyn Loden, author of *Feminine Leadership*)

- He has his priorities straight; she's just playing hard-to-get.

- He's a man of action; she's impulsive.

- He's a family man; she has too many outside distractions.

- He thinks before he acts; she can't make up her mind.

- He tells it like it is; she's too direct.

- He makes things happen; she's lucky.

- He has good ideas; she operates on intuition.

  (Source: Kathleen Kelley Reardon, author of *They Don't Get It, Do They?*)

Pouf!

One afternoon, I caught an early train from Grand Central to Connecticut and sat in the five-togethers, a group of seats occupied in rush hour by bridge players. Scrunched up against the window, working on a needlepoint bluebird, was another woman professionally attired (and professionally tired). We nodded wordlessly, and I opened my newspaper. Before the train left the station, we were joined by two men with overstuffed attaché cases, from which they each pulled a yellow legal pad.

"What've you got?" asked one.

"We're going to have to file Chapter 11 on Monday, and I don't need to tell you what that will do to the stock," replied the other.

"We have tomorrow then? I'll let George know."

I shot a sidelong glance at the needlepointer; she caught my look and raised her eyebrows in a "I can't believe what I'm hearing" message.

The men continued to share privileged information from their respective clients: the company in trouble and the significant investor. When the train pulled into Stamford, one of the attorneys rose to disembark, saying, "Paul, thanks. I'm glad we had a chance to talk privately."

When I was a child I wished I was invisible. Now, I am a woman. Pouf! My wish has come true.

—**Wendy Reid Crisp, Director, National Association of Female Executives, and author of *Do As I Say, Not As I Did***

I was optimistic, but I also expected it to be dif-
ficult. I couldn't close my eyes to the possibility
of bias and discrimination. Prejudice is not the
American way, but there are still individuals
who have those feelings. I had three strikes
against me — I was a woman, I was nonwhite,
and I was a foreigner. No one likes to be the vic-
tim of bias, but it can be a great motivator. I
didn't allow that to get in my way. I would say
to a potential customer, "If you give me a
chance, you won't be sorry." Then when you do
a great job, the bias starts to melt away.

—Kavelle Bajaj, President, I-Net

The Talking Dog Phenomenon

MY FRIEND SHERRY MAY EARNED her divinity degree some thirty-five years ago, long before it was common for women to be ordained. She told me about the first sermon she gave as a guest minister at someone else's church. "A woman in the pulpit giving a sermon is a bit like a talking dog," she said. "People aren't so impressed by what the dog says as they are by the fact that the dog talks at all!"

I recalled Sherry's parable of the talking dog a few years ago when I was hired to conduct training seminars for an automotive manufacturer. Twenty-two people were hired to work on this project — twenty-one men and me. Our job was to travel around the country in teams, conducting product-knowledge training for car salespeople. The manufacturer was launching a new line of small trucks and wanted to ensure that the sales force knew enough about the trucks to sell them effectively. As the twenty-two trainers gathered together on the first day of our train-the-trainer session, we were told that we would have to take a quiz the next morning to ascertain how much we knew about the new trucks. I panicked. I knew something about cars, but trucks were a whole different ballgame — I knew nothing about trucks! "They're going to fire me, for sure," I thought to myself.

I called my boyfriend that night. "What am I going to do?" I wailed. "Half those guys I'm working with are race car drivers and they know tons more than I do!"

"Calm down," he said. "You'll do fine. You don't have to know everything there is to know about trucks. Nobody is expecting you to know much at all – you're a girl, remember? On that quiz tomorrow, all you have to do is do better than the worst guy."

"Really? Is that the way it works?" I asked, calming down.

"Of course. Trust me, I'm a guy. I know these things," he replied.

I thanked him for his reassurance, and went back to studying the truck handbooks.

The next day my twenty-one teammates and I all took the quiz. I scored above 90 percent, much better than most of the guys. They were impressed with how well I did on the quiz. I thought about Sherry's experience as a woman preacher. "It's the talking dog thing," I surmised.

What I learned from Sherry's talking dog story is that sometimes it can be an advantage being a woman working in a male environment. If you don't do too well, you don't lose points, because the guys didn't expect you to do well in the first place. If you do well, you get extra points because they are surprised.

I share this talking dog story with women as often as I can. It's important for us to remember that while being a woman can be a liability in some work environments, it can also be an asset. Our job as women is to make the most of the asset side of the equation, while minimizing the liability side. Arf! Arf!

*Remember, Ginger Rogers did everything Fred Astaire
did but she did in backwards and in high heels.*

—Faith Whittlesey, U.S. ambassador to Switzerland

Women Mean Business

· From 1987 to 1996, women-owned businesses increased 78 percent to
nearly eight million, generating some $2.3 trillion in annual revenues,
and employing one in four American workers.

(Source: National Association of Women Business Owners)

· In 1997, four states — California (700,500), New York (394,000), Texas
(381,500), and Florida (337,800) — accounted for 33 percent of women-
owned firms.

(Source: U.S. Census Bureau)

· Today, more people are employed by women-owned businesses domes-
tically in the US than were employed by all Fortune 500 corporations
worldwide.

(Source: *Megatrends for Women* by Pat Auburdeen)

I Learned the ABCs of
Work from Other Women

WOMEN'S WORK IS TO...

AFFIRM our own and each other's worth

BE curious and ask good questions

COMMIT ourselves to excellence

DIG deeply into life's mysteries

EXPRESS ourselves authentically

FEEL our fears and rise above them

GIVE 110 percent to life each day

HEED our own intuitive wisdom

INITIATE new projects and possibilities

JUGGLE many roles and duties . . . while making it
    look easy!

KEEP our sense of humor, especially when others have
    lost theirs

LISTEN with love

MANAGE our time effectively

NURTURE relationships at work and at home

OPEN our minds to new ideas; open our lives to new opportunities

PREPARE our children for life

QUESTION authority — think for ourselves

REBOUND from setbacks and failures

SET priorities and reevaluate regularly

TAKE good care of ourselves

UNDERSTAND human nature

VEER away from negative people

WIDEN our perspectives

XPECT positive outcomes

YEARN for and work for peace — in our hearts, in our homes, in our world

ZERO in on what's truly important

My Business, My Self

LYNN AND I WERE AT OUR FAVORITE Thai restaurant one evening, comparing notes about what we liked and didn't like about being self-employed.

"The most important thing I've discovered since I left my corporate job is that building a business is, on one level, about making a living and supporting myself; but on a deeper level it is about building my self," Lynn said. "My self-esteem has always been kind of shaky and very changeable, depending on what was going on in my life. In terms of work, I often felt like I was at the mercy of forces beyond my control. I wasn't in charge of my own destiny, since so much of organizational life is in other people's hands, especially bosses."

"I know exactly what you mean," I nodded. "I've never been too wild about bosses myself."

"The best thing about running my own business is becoming my own boss," she continued. "It is both terrifying and exhilarating. There is no authority figure to turn to for guidance – but at the same time, it forces me to grapple with and solve problems for myself. If things go wrong, there is no one to blame but myself. If things go right, I get to claim the credit!

"In growing my business, I am out here in the big world competing with others, testing my wits and resourcefulness, challenging my creativity, and seeing what I am really made of!"

"I hadn't thought about it in just those terms, but you're right,"

I agreed. "When I left my job at the Los Angeles Times, I wondered, 'Who am I now that I don't have a big, prestigious company behind me? Will anybody return my phone calls? I'm just another consultant and trainer, one of thousands – it's just me out here in the marketplace.' I was terrified."

"Yes, but now it's ten years later and you're still in business!" she said. "Don't you feel great about that? Eighty percent of all new businesses fail in the first two years, and you're still here!"

There is something terrifically empowering about leaving the corporate nest and trying your wings on your own. If you find you can't make it, you can always go find another corporate nest to settle in. If your wings grow strong and you learn to master the wind currents, you can soar as high as your imagination and energy will take you!

Lynn was right – building a business is really about building yourself.

A lot of businesses are being started by women who have been working for idiots for years. They know they can do their boss's job, but they know they will never be given it.

–Jean Denton, Director, British Nuclear Fuels

Dear BJ,

You asked me what I have learned from other women: It's the power of networking and collaboration. I didn't realize how powerful this skill was ... call it networking, call it community service, call it membership, what I know now is that the power of my feminine spirit lies in the connection with other feminine spirits. We are the nurturers of the world. We create the nest. We are responsible for relationships. We are the teachers, the guidance system. We are the heartbeat of the world.

When we work together and can collaborate in business we create partnerships that are beyond our imagination. There is certainly enough business out there for everyone. When we get in a spirit of collaboration and participation in the marketplace with each other ... we are referring people all over the place and in the same light attracting others to our own business!

Warm regards,

Patty Walters, change management consultant

We now know it is possible to press through barriers.
We certainly need unity to face the mounting odds
against us. This is essential and joyful work for women
of color in this country today. Honor your work and that
of your sisters: We are the ones we were waiting for.

> —Leah Wise, author of *We Are the Ones We*
> *Were Waiting For*

What does WORK mean to you?

Wonderful		Wasted
Original		Onerous
Rewarding	*or*	Redundant
Kreative		Krushing

What kind of a JOB do you have?

Joy		Jerks
Of	*or*	On my
Building		Back

8

Getting Good at Getting Along

It is not true that life is one damn
thing after another —
it's one damn thing over and over.

—Edna St. Vincent Millay, *poet*

One of my all-time favorite movies is *Annie Hall*. I love the end, when Woody Allen turns to the camera and tells the audience this story:

> This guy goes to a psychiatrist and says, "Doc, my brother's crazy; he thinks he's a chicken." And the doctor says, "Well, why don't you turn him in?" And the guy says, "I would, but I need the eggs."
>
> Well, I guess that's pretty much how I feel about relationships. You know, they're totally irrational and crazy and absurd and...but I guess we keep going through it... because...most of us need the eggs.

Such is the dilemma in which many of us find ourselves. Dealing with other people can be frustrating, exasperating, and even infuriating...but we still have to deal with them.

Families, neighborhoods, workplaces, churches, hospitals, schools, governments — all are made up of people with whom we need to get along. Just how do we do that?

Some of the most helpful things I've learned from other women involve skills for dealing more effectively with people. This book isn't long enough to include all the tips and tools they've taught me, but I did want to share some especially helpful ones. Try them out for yourself and add the ones you like to your own toolkit of people skills.

The idea is to enjoy "the eggs" without having to walk on eggshells.

Stand for Something

MY DEAR FRIEND LESLIE YERKES and I were at an authors' retreat together, spending the evening in front of a fire, sipping wine, and comparing notes about the women in our families who had been influential in our lives.

"My Gramma Jane was a huge influence on me," Leslie said. "Jane Preston Conaway was her name. She was a study in contrasts — she dressed like a lady and ruled like a man. Her household operated on strict and unbending guidelines. Gramma Jane brooked no waffling when it came to right and wrong. Her first commandment to me was, 'Either you stand for something or you will fall for anything.'"

"Did this relate to any particular situation you were in at the time?" I asked Leslie.

"Well, no," Leslie replied. "Nothing special I can recall. I just remember hearing her say it to me on various occasions — like, this is an important rule — pay attention! I first heard Gramma Jane's commandment when I was younger than ten years old, but I didn't fully understand it until I was in my thirties. As a little girl, my youthful interpretation of her commandment was the obvious: If I didn't have values and live by them, I would find myself falling under the influence of people with strong wills and/or attractive positions in life."

"How did your interpretation change as you grew older?" I asked Leslie.

"As my experiences in life began to form a more lustrous patina on my being," she continued, "I realized that Gramma Jane's commandment held even more for me. You see, I was raised in a time when, according to social norms, a little girl was supposed to like and please everyone — we were supposed to 'be nice.'

"When I got out into the work world, it was not always easy for me to stand up and be counted. Gramma's commandment to 'stand for something' seemed at odds with the broader messages I got from others about 'going along to get along.' In the business world, I encountered all sorts of silliness, lunacy, bureaucratic nonsense, and out-and-out wrong-headedness."

"What did you do?" I asked her.

"When I first confronted these situations, I behaved like the sweet little girl I had been raised to be," Leslie replied. "I opted for social norms — 'Be nice.' But over time, Gramma Jane's words got stronger in my consciousness and I began publicly, yet politely, to disagree, and to stand up for what I thought was right, regardless of what someone might think of me.

"Eventually, I discovered that to 'stand for something' meant that I had to risk being disliked if I chose to follow my values. I became more and more willing to pay that price. When I was true to my values, I could feel comfortable with myself regardless of the opinions of others. For that, I can thank my Gramma Jane."

I nodded. "Sometimes the right decision is not the popular one. But I'll bet people respect you more. Your Gramma Jane was a wise woman, and a strong one, too. Too bad we all didn't have a Gramma Jane!"

Standing in the middle of the road is very dangerous;
you get knocked down by the traffic from both sides.

—Margaret Thatcher, former British Prime Minister

Don't compromise yourself. You're all you've got.

—Janis Joplin, singer/songwriter

Speak up for yourself, or you'll end up a rug.

—Mae West, actress

The four visions my mom left me:

- Always do your best, that's good enough.
- Never throw away your tomorrows worrying about yesterday.
- The day you see the truth and cease to speak is the day you die.
- If you want to be out of the cotton patch, you have to get something in your head.

(Source: Dr. Jocelyn Elders, former U.S. Surgeon General)

Speak for Yourself

WHEN I WAS A LITTLE GIRL, "school" was my favorite game. Even as a toddler, I loved pencils, books, notebooks, pencil boxes, chalk, blackboards, and all the other paraphernalia of a classroom.

Today, "school" is still my favorite game! I love going to seminars and workshops. I love reading books. I love writing, doing research, and learning new things. I'm fortunate that I make my living "playing school" – in an adult environment. I teach seminars, I conduct workshops, and I facilitate group sessions, both large and small. Not only do I read books, I write them, too. I get to have all the school supplies I want – a little girl's dream come true!

Over the years, I've attended many workshops and learned practical people skills. One such seminar, taught by Maria Arapakis, taught me a very useful skill: how to use "I language."

Before taking that seminar, I was very good at using "you language" – statements like, "You hurt my feelings," "You're never around when I need you," "You don't listen when I'm talking to you," and, "You don't love me." I used "you language" in my personal life and at work, and it seemed to me that everyone else did the same.

Maria pointed out the problem with "you language": it makes the other person defensive. Using "you" is the verbal equivalent of pointing an accusatory finger at the other person. Imagine having a finger wagged in your face – that's what it feels like to be listening to someone talking about "you."

When someone is accusing me, making me wrong, I have only two choices: (1) I can instantly build an emotional wall to defend myself, or (2) I can counter-attack and throw some "you's" back at my accuser. That response leaves us both unhappy and defensive. It's a lose-lose situation.

Maria showed me the brilliance of using "I language" instead. Instead of accusing, I describe with these statements: "I feel hurt when I hear comments like that," "I'm disappointed when my birthday is forgotten by someone I love," or, "I feel like my work is devalued when I don't get any feedback." See the difference? I am describing how I feel, what I perceive, and how things affect me, keeping the focus on myself, not on you. That enables you to hear me, because your defenses are not up.

This simple technique has helped me enormously in both my personal and professional life – and sometimes in extremely diffi-cult situations.

Several ago I had a colleague named Fred. We both worked at a university in Southern California and reported to the same boss. Fred fancied himself as something of a ladies' man and was an incorrigible flirt. He often made suggestive comments and inap-propriate jokes when we were working together. I just shrugged it off as Fred being a jerk. One day he crossed the line – he got annoyed with me for something, and in a mock huff he said, "Hmpf! Well, see if I ogle you anymore!"

"That's it!" I thought to myself, offended. "What an ass! Now he's gone too far." I thought about the situation carefully for the next week and talked it over with a couple of girlfriends. I didn't want to complain to my boss about sexual harassment, and I didn't want to take it to Human Resources. I wanted to see if I could handle the situation on my own.

I called Fred and asked if I could schedule a meeting with him. "I have a problem that I'd like your help with," I told him, which was the absolute truth.

During the meeting, I introduced the issue by saying, "Fred, I'm having a problem with our work relationship and I want to enlist your help in solving the problem."

"Sure," he replied, clearly eager to help.

Recalling what Maria had taught me about using "I language," I took a deep breath and began. "Here's the situation, Fred. You and I have to work together and I think we both want the same thing — a relationship of mutual trust and respect."

Fred nodded as he listened.

"But sometimes in the course of our conversations, I hear things that don't make me feel good," I continued. "I hear off-color jokes and I get embarrassed. I experience flirtation, and I feel like I'm not being taken seriously. When I hear suggestive comments, I feel like I'm being looked at as a potential date or sexual partner, not as a professional colleague. In short, I get uncomfortable when we're working together sometimes, and it's a problem. It doesn't work for me. Can you help me solve the problem?"

The look on his face was one of surprise and concern. "I'm so sorry," he began. "I had no idea you felt like that. I thought I was paying you compliments. I thought you liked the flirting!"

"Well, I didn't think it was your intent to make me uncomfortable," I replied, "but sometimes there's a big gap between intent and impact." I wanted to give him the benefit of the doubt and to let him find a way to handle my concern gracefully.

"Of course it wasn't," he said. "I'm so sorry my comments made you feel bad. It'll never happen again."

It never did. We concluded our conversation, I went back to my office, and the problem was solved. "I language" worked. Fred was able to hear me without getting defensive, and I got what I wanted – he changed his behavior.

Since then, I have used "I language" in hundreds of other situations – with neighbors whose barking dog was keeping me awake at night; with contractors whose work was not up to par; even with my family members. It's a simple, highly effective tool for solving problems with other people.

Does "I language" work 100 percent of the time? Of course not, nothing works 100 percent of the time when human beings are involved. But it works at least 90 percent of the time, maybe more. It definitely works 100 percent better than the "you language" I had been using before!

The bottom line is that I have to be clear about what I want. If what I want is to be right and make the other person wrong, and I don't care about results, then any language will do just fine. If what I want is to change someone's behavior and solve a problem, then "I language" is the way to go. It works.

In a "you or me" world, the job is to get enough
and if I get more than I need, I give some to you, but
never do I give you the power to get it.

In a "you and me" world, the job is to make it work for
everyone with no one left out.

—Lynne W. Twist, co-founder of the Pachamama
Alliance and author of *The Soul of Money*

Simple Guidelines for a Life That Works

- Show Up
- Pay Attention
- Tell Your Truth
- Don't Be Attached to the Outcome

—Angeles Arrien, author of *The Four-fold Way*

Everything I Need to Know About Communication I've Learned from Other Women

WHAT MAKES FOR GOOD COMMUNICATION?

Clear, simple words

Open minds

Mutual commitment to understand

Mutual commitment to be understood

Unambiguous meaning

Nonjudgmental words and tone

Integrity of intention

Congruence of verbal message and body language

Articulate, authentic expression

Timely, appropriate feedback

Intent to listen and learn

Ongoing clarification and re-clarification

Nondefensive attitude

Don't Take It Personally

YEARS AGO I HAD A HIGH-POWERED literary agent. She was smart, talented, and successful. I was fortunate that she took an interest in my manuscript, because it is just as hard to find a good agent as it is to find a good publisher. I was grateful to have Irene representing me, but she is not a warm, fuzzy person – she is more cool, aloof, and private. She speaks deliberately and carefully, with little emotion. Even when she likes something, her response seems tepid.

I spent a year working with Irene on revising the manuscript to get it in shape to send out to publishers. She essentially served as editor as well as agent. I would send her the manuscript with my most recent changes, and she would read it over and mark it up with a red pen, indicating areas that still needed more work. Then she'd send it back to me. Reading through her comments, I would get my feelings hurt, cry, get depressed, and not be able to work on it for two weeks. Then I would come out of my funk and get back to work, making the required changes. We went on like this for months.

I recall complaining to my friend Nancy about it one day. Nancy is the person who had recommended Irene in the first place. "I don't think she's the right agent for me," I whined to Nancy. "She's so picky and critical – I don't think she's ever going to happy with this book. She never tells me my work is good; she doesn't tell me my ideas are wonderful; all she does is point out what needs to be changed. I think I should find a new agent."

"Really?" Nancy responded. "Let me ask you, are her suggestions good ones? Is the manuscript getting stronger?"

"Well, yes," I replied. "But she hurts my feelings. She's so cool and aloof."

"She's not supposed to be your mother," Nancy chuckled. "This is business. She doesn't have to love you – she just has to help you get your manuscript into shape so she can sell it. If you want someone to jump up and down and tell you you're wonderful, call your Mom . . . or get a dog."

"Easy for you to say," I grumbled. "Irene's your friend. I'll bet she doesn't hurt your feelings."

"Get over it. She's doing her job and you're turning it into something personal," Nancy scolded me. "I think you should stick with her as an agent because you need to learn that it isn't personal – it's business."

Nancy was absolutely right. I hung in there with Irene and worked through all the emotions that came up during our interactions. I came to see that what was really going on was unfinished business with my parents, particularly my dad, who had always set extremely high standards for me. I felt like I was never good enough. Irene was simply hitting those old "critical parent" buttons.

What Nancy taught me was that my difficulties with Irene really had nothing to do with Irene at all! It was old business – old baggage with my parents, still hanging around from childhood.

Continuing to work with Irene enabled me to work through all those childish expectations of wanting her to be the warm, effusive, unconditionally loving parent I never had. It's not Irene's job to do that. Nor is it anyone else's job.

Thanks to Nancy's insights and coaching, today I can interact with all different kinds of people, and have little or no trouble. I can handle their criticisms, their tough standards, and their cool personal style. I can establish good relationships with people who are difficult, demanding, prickly, and even rude and obnoxious. Who they are and how they act has nothing to do with me – they're just being themselves.

It was an important lesson for life: Don't take it personally.

I bear no grudges. I have a mind that retains nothing.

—Bette Midler, singer, actress

Love your enemy – it will drive him nuts.

—Eleanor Doan, educator

A Complaint Is a Gift

"WHAT A CONCEPT!" I marveled to myself as I read my friend Janelle Barlow's book, *A Complaint Is a Gift.* It's a business book about customer service and the importance of getting feedback, especially negative feedback, from customers. Janelle asserts that complaints are not problems to be avoided – complaints are actually gifts to be welcomed!

Complaints are important for several reasons, Janelle writes:

- You don't know how to improve your product or service if you don't know what's wrong.
- Customer complaints can give you ideas for new products and services.
- Complaints give you valuable information about what's important to people, and what they're willing to spend money on.

Complaints also tell you that the customer still wants to do business with you – she still cares about the relationship she has with your company, and she wants you to fix the problem so she can continue to do business with you. Most customers don't complain – they just take their business elsewhere because they've given up hope of getting what they need from you.

The problem is, most people think that customer complaints are bad. They mistakenly think that no complaints means no problems. As long as you're in business, you will always have problems.

The important thing to focus on is how you handle those problems when they occur.

That's why a complaint is really a gift. Just like we thank someone who gives us a birthday gift, we should thank someone who brings us a complaint. They have given us something valuable, something useful, and something that can help make our business stronger and more profitable — we should treat their complain as the gift that it really is.

As I read Janelle's book, I found myself thinking that her idea applied to personal relationships, too. I thought about the different ways that complaints come into our lives: our parents complain about some aspect of our behavior; our lovers complain when they feel neglected; or our friends complain if we have a misunderstanding. Complaints are simply a normal part of what it means to live in relationships with other people.

After reading Janelle's book, I started reacting differently when someone in my life complained to me. Of course, sometimes I would forget that a complaint is a gift, and I reacted defensively. When I could catch myself and remind myself of Janelle's advice, I could make the interaction a learning experience rather than a battle. I could use their complaint to make our relationship better, rather than let the complaint tear us apart.

If someone in my life has a complaint about me, I can be reassured by the fact that they are at least still talking to me. That tells me that they still care about our relationship and they want to make it better. If they stop talking to me, that's when I should worry — that's when they've given up on the relationship.

In treating complaints as gifts in my personal life, I have adapted Janelle's teachings about handling customer complaints:

1. I thank the person for his complaint. I tell him how much I appreciate his taking the time to tell me about his problem.

2. I tell him why I'm thanking him — because I care about our relationship and his complaint gave me an opportunity to address anything that isn't working between us.

3. I apologize for the fact that he is unhappy. I don't assume guilt or say that it is my fault, I simply say, "I'm sorry you're unhappy about this."

4. I promise to do whatever I can to help solve the problem.

5. I sometimes ask for more information, clarification, or specifics, so that I can fully understand his unhappiness.

6. I take whatever steps I can to correct the problem — focusing on things that are within my control. If something is out of my control, I explain that. If something really has nothing to do with me at all, this is the point in the discussion when we are most likely to discover that.

7. I ask him if he feels his complaint is being addressed. If not, we go back to the beginning of the process.

8. I try to learn from the situation — I learn new things about myself, about him, and about our relationship.

Most important of all, I always emphasize what I *can* do rather than what I *can't.* I look for what is possible rather than telling him what is impossible. Pointing out what I can't do simply makes us both more frustrated.

This "complaint is a gift" notion is not one that comes naturally to me — nor probably to anyone. None of us likes to hear negative feedback, particularly from people we care about. If we can hear what's behind the complaint — the desire to fix something that's hurting the other person — then we can see how their complaint really is a gift!

The change of one simple behavior can affect other behaviors and thus change many things.

—Jean Baer, author of *How to Be an Assertive (Not Aggressive) Woman in Life, in Love, and on the Job*

I have a simple philosophy.
Fill what's empty.
Empty what's full.
Scratch where it itches.

—Alice Roosevelt Longworth, President Theodore Roosevelt's daughter

Dear BJ,

The most important thing I learned from another woman is,

"Life is not about being comfortable."

My dear friend Linda Parker responded to my whining several years ago with that simple and profound statement. I have called on it time and again to gather the courage to move forward into that uncomfortable zone; that is the only way to reach the higher zone.

It can be applied to ordering a new food in a restaurant, to stepping into a new restaurant in the first place, to taking your first backpacking trip, to dealing with conflict and misunderstandings, to quitting a job in which you are limited, or to accepting a date with a man whose smile dazzles you.

Warmly,
Brenda McCord

Know Your Audience!

MY NEIGHBOR PATTI RILEY is a business communication professor at USC who conducts training seminars on presentation skills. She begins each seminar with a dedication to Gen. George S. Custer, who had no idea what he was riding into at Little Big Horn; the Indians slaughtered him and his entire cavalry command. Patti's motto is, "Know your audience." Patti's advice is not just important for making presentations and fighting battles – it is good advice for dealing with other people on a day-to-day basis.

Patti's words of wisdom call to my mind the case of two senior executives at the *Los Angeles Times* with whom I worked in the late 1980s. John and Barry (not their real names) both reported to Paul (not his real name, either), who was the publisher of the paper. Barry, who was the senior vice president of operations, had a great relationship with Paul. Barry always seemed to be able to get his projects approved and his budgets okayed. John, on the other hand, always seemed to be in trouble with Paul. John was bright and talented – he hadn't become the chief financial officer by being a schlump – but for some reason, he always seemed to be shooting himself in the foot.

One day, John approached Barry and asked him for his help. "I always seem to be on Paul's blacklist, and you seem to be the golden boy. What am I doing wrong?" asked John.

"Simple," Barry replied. "Paul's a very moody guy – everybody knows that. One day he's relaxed and open; the next day he can be dark and brooding. You never know from one day to the next what kind of mood he'll be in. But it's easy to find out what kind of mood he's in by looking at his face. He's absolutely transparent — his face is an open book.

"Whenever I need to see Paul about something, I go down to his office with two folders under my arm. One folder contains what I really want to talk about; the other is something simple that I just need a quick signature on.

"Paul has a big office, and his desk is all the way across the room from the door. So, as I come through his office door, I have plenty of time to size up his mood before I get to his desk.

"If I see he's in a foul mood, I pull out the folder that's quick and simple, lay it in front of him, and say, 'Just need a quick signature here, Paul.' He signs it and I'm outta there.

"If I see he's in a good mood, then I pull out the folder with the real thing I want to talk with him about and ask him for some time to discuss it.

"It's simple, really. I know my audience."

The point my friend Patti makes in emphasizing the importance of "knowing your audience" is that the world is all about relationships. Not just relationships between bosses and employees, but relationships between co-workers, relationships between friends, relationships with family members, and with neighbors. To paraphrase a well-known 1992 campaign slogan: "It's relationships, stupid." Life is about relationships.

Patti taught me that if I want to have effective relationships with people, then I need to know my audience. Who is that other person I am interacting with? The more I listen, ask questions, study, observe, analyze, reflect, and understand about the people in my life, the more effective I will be in my relationships with them. If I do my homework and learn about the other person, then I am more likely to get what I need or want from him or her.

Poor Custer – he blew it with the Indians. Poor John – he blew it with his boss. The former lost his life, and the latter lost favor. Too bad they didn't know my friend Patti. She could have told them about the importance of knowing your audience!

The real art of conversation is not only to say the right thing in the right place, but to leave unsaid the wrong thing at the tempting moment.

—Dorothy Nevill, British author, social hostess

Courage comes from wanting to say it well;
security comes from knowing you can say it well;
confidence comes from having said it well.

—Anonymous

Getting Off to a Good Start

MY FRIEND JUDITH SEGAL moved to Los Angeles about twenty years ago, leaving her home in Montreal. She needed to buy insurance, so she went to the only place she could think of — a big company with a well-known name. The insurance salesman was the stereotypical type you see in the movies — slick and smelling of too much after-shave. She bought her insurance and went on her way. The next thing she knew, this guy showed up at her house, trying to sell her even more insurance. She told him no, but he didn't give up easily. He pestered her for a good six weeks before he finally gave up and left her alone.

Several years later, Judith was working on her Ph.D. dissertation studying the traits and skills of successful businesswomen. She talked to lots of people and compiled a list of accomplished women to interview. One of those was Kim Bradley, who was very successful in the insurance business. Kim greeted Judith warmly when Judith arrived at Kim's office for their interview, inviting her to sit and talk over a cup of coffee.

"Have you ever dealt with anyone in the insurance business before?" Kim asked.

Judith hesitated. "Well, I have bought insurance in the past...," she started, but she didn't want to be rude to Kim by speaking ill of insurance salespeople.

"Did you have a good experience?" Kim pressed for more information.

"Well, no, to be honest, I didn't," Judith replied. She told Kim the story of the pushy insurance guy.

Kim listened carefully, nodded sympathetically, and then said, "Gosh, that sounds just terrible. I'm sorry you had that experience. Let me tell you how I work, and how I am different from that insurance salesperson...." She proceeded to explain her style and approach to doing business.

That was a very important conversation for Judith. Not only did she learn a lot about Kim's skills and how she became successful, Judith also took a page from her book and started using the same introductory technique with her own clients.

Today, whenever she meets a potential client, she begins the conversation with, "Have you ever worked with a consultant before?" This question enables the person to discuss whatever bad experiences or negative feelings right up front. It enables Judith to see immediately what's on this person's mind as well as his or her unspoken fears or concerns. She can deal with his or her past experiences with the simple statement, "Let me tell you how what I do is different from the other consultants you've dealt with...."

As Judith told me this story, it occurred to me that this same tool could also be used in personal relationships. For instance, on a first date with someone I can ask, "Have you ever dated anyone from an online dating service before?" After he tells me his experiences, I can say, "Let me tell you how I am different from those women." In meeting new neighbors, I can ask, "Have you ever lived in a community like this before?" After hearing their experiences, I can tell them, "Let me tell you how our community is special."

Kim taught Judith and Judith taught me this wonderful technique for getting relationships off to a good start. I'm going to try it with my next book editor... "So, have you worked with authors before? ... Let me tell you how I am different from those other authors...."

Class is an aura of confidence that is being sure without being cocky. Class has nothing to do with money. Class never runs scared. It is self-discipline and self-knowledge. It's the sure-footedness that comes with having proved you can meet life.

—Ann Landers, advice columnist

Dear BJ,

Simply "ask," "ask," "ask," is what I've learned from my great friend Lynne Boutross. "You can't ask for that...," "I could never request...," "They would never let me...." Lynn blew all my beliefs right out of the water. She taught me that all things are possible, but first you've got to step out and "ask." From Lynn I've dared to request a different table at a restaurant, returned food that wasn't right, returned merchandise that had a problem, and asked for special consideration in a variety of circumstances. Lynne's example is not one of a wild banshee woman, but of sound, self-assured "putting it out there." She often gets what she wants because she's good at letting others know what it is. It's a great lesson to learn.

Sincerely,
Wendy Menjou
flower essence consultant

9

Thorns Among the Roses

All that is necessary to break the spell
of inertia and frustration is this:
Act as if it were impossible to fail.
That is the talisman, the formula,
the command of right-about-face
which turns us from failure
towards success.

—*Dorothea Brande, author of*
Becoming a Writer

omeone wise once said, "Circumstances don't make a person's character, they reveal it." This is especially true when life gets tough. Disappointment and disaster show us what we're really made of. Struggle and suffering test our physical, emotional, and spiritual strength. We grow as human beings in the facing and overcoming of difficulties, and we more fully become the remarkable women we are capable of being. As Maya Angelou wrote, "You may encounter many defeats, but you must not be defeated. In fact, the encountering may be the very experience which creates the vitality and the power to endure."

We respond to defeats and difficulties in many different ways. Some of us are stoics, drawing from deep inner strength to walk through dark days. Many of us reach out to our friends for sustenance and support. We cry, we talk, we hug, we pray, we write in letters or journals, we gather together in support groups, and we send cards and e-mails of encouragement. We learn from one another how to survive — and sometimes even thrive — in the face of problems we dreaded and feared. We are women. We are strong.

Doing What We Fear We Cannot Do

SUE HALL AND I HAD LOST touch over the years. I always liked her, but somehow our friendship lagged as our lives took us in different directions. I can't remember who finally got in touch whom, but one of us did, and we finally decided to make a lunch date — both of us eager to catch up with each other's lives.

I had heard through mutual friends that Sue had had cancer a few years ago, but when we met for lunch she looked the picture of health. I was happily surprised.

"How are you feeling?" I asked. "How's your health?"

"Great!" she replied. "It's been over five years now, so I'm a survivor."

"Wow! That's great! I am so happy for you and your family," I told her.

We fell silent for a moment, savoring Sue's victory over the Big C.

I broke the silence: "Did it change your life? Did you learn any of those profound lessons that people often report after a life-threatening illness?"

She thought about it for a minute. "Yes, it did ... something so serious, how could it not?"

I sat back to listen to the rest of her story.

"I found a lump while doing a breast self-exam about six years ago. Being a physician myself, I found it easy to convince myself that it would be a benign breast tumor ... certainly not cancer! In my head, I went over all the features of a benign lump – smooth, easily moveable, soft – and I didn't worry at all about cancer, so thoroughly had I convinced myself that my lump met the criteria for a non-cancerous lump.

"However, I did get myself to a doctor within several weeks. My primary care doctor agreed with my assessment that it was probably 'nothing to worry about,' but of course, we had to get it checked out.

"I went for my mammogram and only when the radiologist brought me in to her office to talk about the results did I become worried. 'Cancer?' I thought. 'I can't have that – I couldn't handle it.'

"The radiologist was concerned enough that she called my primary care doctor. They agreed that I should see a surgeon – immediately. 'That's good,' I thought, 'then I'll find out soon that it's nothing to worry about.'

"About twenty minutes later I arrived in the surgeon's office. As he examined my lump, he commented that he didn't like the feel of it. He wanted to do a needle biopsy right away – as in, right then and there! 'Good,' I thought again, 'I'll find out really soon that it's nothing.' Twenty minutes after the needle aspiration was done, he reentered the examining room and sat down. 'You have a malignant tumor,' he said.

"My next thought was 'Well, okay, but it can't have spread. I couldn't handle it if it had spread. I just simply couldn't deal with chemotherapy.' Cancer requiring surgery was one thing, and even radiation probably wouldn't be so bad … but chemotherapy? I wanted no part of it.

"Two days after my surgery, I found out that the tumor had spread to one lymph node. Guess what? Chemotherapy was next on the agenda. While going through all of this, I joined a support group at the hospital. During one of the first sessions, one of the women gave advice to another woman who was having trouble dealing with her fears of the future. The woman said, 'Half of what you worry about won't happen, and the other half you can handle.'

"As I reflected on her statement over the months, I found that it was true. I could handle what came my way – because there was no other choice!

"I have embraced this statement since then, and have used it to help my children cope with changes in their lives as well. We all have strengths of which we are perhaps not fully aware, and we are all capable of rising to the occasion and even showing our most beautiful and complete selves. I no longer say, 'I could never handle that' about anything! My bout with cancer and that other woman's wisdom taught me that I can handle whatever I have to."

Sue looked up from salad and smiled at me: "So, did I answer your question?"

How Do You Handle ADVERSITY?

Persist no matter what.

Endure discomfort.

Refuse to give up.

Steadfastly hold to your beliefs and values.

Envision triumph.

Very consistently keep at it.

Express gratitude for Divine love and support.

Request help from other people.

Enjoy and celebrate every tiny bit of progress!

I gain strength, courage, and confidence by every experience in which I must stop and look fear in the face.... I say to myself, "I've lived through this and can take the next thing that comes along."... We must do the thing we think we cannot do.

—Eleanor Roosevelt, former First Lady

Life shrinks or expands in proportion to one's courage.

—Anaïs Nin, novelist, diarist

When "I Do" Turns into "I Can't"

"MY MARRIAGE WAS LIKE the parable of the boiled frog," Mona Lynne told me. "You know, if you put a frog in a pan of room temperature water, he's happy. Then you put the pan on the stove and turn up the heat, a little bit at a time. The frog keeps adjusting to the gradual temperature change and doesn't even notice it . . . until it's too late, the water boils, and he dies. That's how my marriage was — it just got worse and worse during the twelve years Steve and I were together, and I kept adjusting so that I didn't really see how bad it was until I ultimately got out of the marriage.

"I'm a very religious woman, living in the South, and I was raised to believe that when you say, 'I do' to those marriage vows, you mean it. You're supposed to find a way to make it work, to honor your commitment to your partner and your faith. All the time I was married, I kept thinking if I could just adjust myself, be a better wife, be a better mother, that if I could just do something more to keep him happy, then everything would be all right."

"When did the problems start?" I asked.

"When we started having children," Mona Lynne replied. "I noticed that Steve was pretty hard on our two boys, even when they were just little guys. He didn't hit them, but he was rough. He was critical of them, and of me. He was a perfectionist, and it seemed like nothing was ever good enough for him."

"Did you try counseling?" I asked.

"Yes, we did," she answered, "but after a few visits, Steve

wouldn't go anymore. He said I was the one with the problem, and so I was the one who needed therapy."

"That must have been hard," I said.

"Yes, it was. I tried everything I could to make my marriage work. Finally one day, I asked Steve, 'What do you want from me? What would it take to make you happy?' And his answer gave me what I needed to know. He said he wanted me to get a job – that he was tired of me staying home and taking care of the kids. (Never mind that I was earning money by taking care of three other children too – I had *five* kids in my home!) He said he wanted the house to be immaculate and in perfect order; he wanted at least one 'real meal' a day – no hot dogs, pizza, or sandwiches. He wanted me to keep him happy in bed, and he wanted me to never leave the house without him."

"Quite a list!" I responded.

"Yes, it was, and he wasn't kidding. In his mind, that's what he wanted me to be," Mona Lynne said.

"Sounds like he wanted three women – not one," I said. "A career woman; a perfect homemaker and mother; and a charming companion."

"Three or five, I don't know," she answered. "All I knew was that I could never do it. And I told him so. I saw then that it was impossible – there was no way this marriage was going to work. So I took my children and left."

"How did you survive your divorce?" I asked her.

"Well, I did several things," she said, "I relied a lot on my faith, and I turned to the Lord for help. I relied a lot on my family, too. The whole time I was married, I never let anyone in my family know that there was trouble, so everyone was taken by surprise when I left my husband. But once I told my parents and the rest of my family the story about what had been going on, they were very supportive. My mother took care of my boys, who were four and six when we split up, while I took a full-time job.

"My counselor was very helpful, and I continued to see her for years. I couldn't have made it without her. She helped me see what my part in the divorce was – how I had permitted Steve to treat me badly, I had never drawn any boundaries or taken care of myself. She recommended that I keep as many positive male role models around as I could, so that my boys would have more than their father to look to for guidance on how to be a male. She also recommended that I put the boys in sports, anything where they could run and run, to give them a healthy outlet for any anger and resentment. So I did, I put them in soccer."

"Sounds like you got some good advice," I commented.

"Yes, I was very lucky. It was pretty awful, both in the marriage and afterward, but I made the right choice," Mona Lynne said. "You know how some people say that they stay married for the sake of the kids? Well, I had to *leave* for the sake of the kids. I was afraid that if I stayed, it would only get worse. I feared for the physical safety of my boys and myself. But even more importantly, I was terrified that they would turn out to be just like their dad. I saw the same pattern of abusive behavior is Steve's dad, in his brother, and in his grandfather. I knew that it would just get passed on to my boys. I had to get them away from Steve, or their fate was sealed."

"So, how are things today?" I asked her.

"Really good," she replied with a smile. "My boys are now twenty and sixteen, and they are so wonderful. My twenty-year-old has a girlfriend, and you should see how nice he treats her. It makes me so happy. I have not remarried; I don't even date very often. And when I do date, I often don't let the men come to the house – I meet them somewhere else, because I don't want my kids to get attached to another man and then have it not work out. That's not fair to them. My main focus has been on raising my boys and doing whatever it takes to give them a good start in life."

Mona Lynne's story made me think about my own divorce and how I wished that someone had given me the advice that her therapist gave her. Keeping my son in sports, giving him lots of healthy male role models, being careful about bringing dates and boyfriends home, and relying on faith and family – all those things would have made such a difference when I got my divorce twenty years ago. Mona Lynne was fortunate – she had wise people around her to coach and guide her – she didn't try to go it alone. She knew that it takes a village to raise a child ... *and* to help a family through divorce.

Mona Lynne's story taught me once again the lesson of community. Humans are social creatures, and we do best when we stick together. The myth of the rugged individual is just that – a myth. What's that old song that Barbra Streisand used to sing?

"People ... people who need people, are the luckiest people in the world." Mona Lynne taught me what it means to be lucky.

I know God won't give me anything I can't handle.
I just wish he didn't trust me so much.

—**Mother Teresa, Catholic nun, humanitarian**

Learning to Just *Be*
with the Darkness

"I'M SO DEPRESSED," I told my friend Renata. "First, I got myself into this disastrous relationship with my boss. Then it blew up because he wants to marry me, and I told him I wouldn't marry him. Now he's making my life miserable, and I have to leave my job – I can't stand it anymore. Boy, when I make a mistake, I make a big one! I've managed to make a mess of my personal life and my work life, all at the same time!"

"What are you doing about it?" Renata asked me.

"I'm trying everything...," I replied, "job hunting, getting therapy, avoiding my boss, throwing myself into my work. But I can't seem to get out of this depression. I feel like I'm in quicksand – the harder I work to try to fix things, the more stuck I get."

Renata nodded sagely. She always seemed so centered, so grounded. I hoped she might have some good advice.

"Sometimes, I've learned, the best you can do is just let the darkness overtake you," she said gently. "You won't die from it, though you might feel like you want to die, to end your misery. But nothing lasts forever, and this won't either. It'll pass."

Renata had studied the works of Carl Jung, and brought her Jungian sensibilities to her work as a consultant and to her personal life as well. I hadn't expected the kind of advice she gave me, but it seemed to make sense – particularly in light of the futility of everything else I'd tried.

Renata's advice reminded me of advice my father had given me when he was teaching me to body-surf as a little girl. "If you get hit by a big wave and it pushes you under, don't try to fight it – you'll just make yourself exhausted and the wave is much stronger than you are," he said. "Instead, let yourself go limp, and just roll with the wave. Hold your breath; let yourself be tumbled around; and know that the wave will lose strength as it rolls toward shore, and you'll be pushed to the surface again where you can breathe."

Dad and Renata were both right. The surf doesn't push me under forever – the wave tumbles me around, and then I bob up to the surface again. Depression doesn't keep me down forever, either. If I can see no clear solution or quick fix, I just let the sadness run its course, and then I bob up to the top again – back to normal.

I don't know if Carl Jung ever went body-surfing ... nowhere in his writings does he say, "Surf's up, dude!" But he clearly understood the concept ... as did my friend Renata.

To live is to suffer. To survive is to find some meaning in the suffering.

—Roberta Flack, singer/songwriter

Women and Depression

Studies have consistently found that women's risk of depression exceeds that of men by a ratio of 2 to 1… Approximately 70 percent of all prescriptions for antidepressants are given to women, but often with improper diagnosis and monitoring. Depression in women is misdiagnosed at least 30-50 percent of the time.

(Source: American Psychological Association's National Task Force on Women and Depression, 1992)

I try to fill the emptiness deep inside me with Cheetos, but I am still depressed. Only now my fingers are stained orange. I am blue. And I am orange.

—Karen Salmansohn, author of *How to Succeed in Business Without a Penis*

Women Need Chocolate

When the going gets tough, women reach for chocolate. Study after study shows that chocolate is the number one food craving of women (followed by bread and ice cream). The American Dietetic Association reports that fully 40 percent of all women crave chocolate. But why? What is it with our chocolate connection?

I learned the answer from Debra Waterhouse, who's written a book on the subject. She explains that chocolate is the drug of choice for women because of its effects on our brain chemistry and our blood sugar levels. Chocolate is 50 percent fat, which is a mood elevator. Chocolate is also 40 percent sugar, which a mood stabilizer and calm-enhancer. So there you have it. Chocolate is legal, inexpensive, easy to get, and effective – the perfect drug. No wonder there are so many chocaholics in the world!

It'll-Cure-Whatever-Ails-You Fudge

Ingredients

    12 marshmallows

    2 cups sugar

    1 small can of evaporated milk (⅔ cup)

    1 pkg. chocolate chips (6 oz.)

    1 stick of butter (8 oz.)

    1 tsp. vanilla

    1 cup chopped nuts (optional)

continued

Directions

Cut marshmallows into pieces (or use miniature marshmallows).

Mix with sugar and milk in a saucepan.

Cook over medium heat, stirring constantly, until marshmallows melt.

Cook mixture exactly 7 minutes, continuing to stir constantly.

Remove from heat; add chocolate chips, butter, and vanilla.

Stir until well blended and smooth.

Add nuts, if desired.

Pour into a buttered pie pan or dish.

Let it cool for a little while, then cut into squares. If you're really depressed, forget cutting it – just grab a spoon and dig in.

If there's any fudge left when you're done, cover the dish with clear plastic wrap or foil, and store at room temperature.

Seen on a woman's T-shirt:

Just hand over the chocolate, and no one will get hurt!

Research tells us that 14 out of any 10 individuals like chocolate.

—Sandra Boynton, artist, author

Always serve too much hot fudge sauce on hot fudge sundaes. It makes people overjoyed, and puts them in your debt.

—Judith Olney, food writer famous for her
chocolate buttermilk cake

Anyone Want to Move to Switzerland?

American consumption of chocolate has been increasing steadily over the past two decades, from 8 pounds per person in 1983 to 12 pounds per person in 2002. By comparison, the Swiss eat 22 pounds of the sweet stuff per year.

(Source: *Los Angeles Times*)

Lessons in Suffering and Compassion

MY FRIEND PEARL is eighty-six years old. Herb, her husband of forty-seven years, died last year. I called her recently to see how she was doing.

"You know, BJ," she began, "a few years, ago one of my neighbors lost her husband. They had been married twenty or thirty years, I'm not sure. I really didn't know her too well. I sent her a sympathy card when her husband died, but I had no idea what she was going through — I didn't know how awful it is to lose your life partner. This past year without Herb has been so hard. If I knew then what I know now, I would have done a lot more for my neighbor when her husband died. I just had no idea...."

Pearl's comment made me think about how little I know of other people's suffering. I have not lost someone close to me (yet). I have not had to battle a life-threatening disease. I do not live with chronic pain. I have not been homeless. I'm not on welfare or food stamps. I've never been assaulted or burglarized. But I know people who have. How can I begin to understand their suffering, their pain, their distress?

I can't tell them, "I know how you feel," because I don't. Only someone who's been there really understands how they feel. I can only imagine their suffering. And I'm sure that whatever I imagine is only a fraction of what they are experiencing.

The only thing I can do in the face of someone else's suffering is to be compassionate, to provide a witness to their pain, and to offer them whatever they need from me. I can listen. I can ask, "How can I help you?" Even if their answer is, "You can't help — there's nothing you can do," I can still look for ways to let them know that I care, and that I'm available.

Most of all, I can love them and I can pray for them. Sometimes that's all I can do . . . but that's still a lot.

You don't develop courage by being happy in your relationships every day. You develop it by surviving difficult times and challenging adversity.

—Barbara De Angelis, author, relationship expert

We could never learn to be brave and patient
if there were only joy in the world.

—Helen Keller, author, lecturer

A Reason to Live

"I SAT THERE ON THE BATHROOM FLOOR, fingering the razor blade I had gotten out of the medicine cabinet," Anastasia told me. "My life was a mess, and I wanted out of my misery. 'Why not just end it all?' I asked myself. My marriage was over, I had no job, and my daughter was acting out at school again, after having been expelled from two other schools already that year. I was drinking too much — I was twenty-nine years old, and everything I thought my life would be by that age was shot. I had no money, no education, no future. I felt totally lost."

Anastasia was telling me her story late one October evening, as we lingered over cappuccino at a favorite local restaurant. We were both in a reflective mood, and we were sharing our thoughts on the meaning of life and other Big Questions. "So why didn't you end it all?" I asked her.

"That was the most important night of my entire life," Anastasia replied. "I was standing on the edge of the abyss, peering over the edge, contemplating letting myself fall into the darkness that lay before me. I knew that I was at a decision point — I had to find a reason to live, or I would die that night.

"I don't know how much time I spent sitting there with that razor blade," she continued. "Maybe it was an hour, maybe it was half the night — I don't remember. All I remember was drifting in some kind of weird state, toying with the blade while I reviewed my life. Was there any reason at all to hang in there?

"Finally the answer came to me. It was like a bubble rising slowly from some deep place to the surface of my consciousness."

"And . . . ?" I asked gently.

"The answer was other people." She looked me directly in the eye. "I saw this image of a spider web in my mind – it was a web of interconnectedness, with everyone I knew connected to everyone else. I had to stick around because I was connected to so many other people, and I couldn't bail out on them. I owed them my presence. What would it do to my daughter if her mother killed herself? How would that scar her for life? It would devastate my mother – I could imagine her just crumbling at the news. I thought about my friends, my co-workers, my neighbors – all the people in my life who would be affected by my death. I couldn't hurt them all like that."

"How have you felt since then?" I asked.

"My life has changed," she answered, "but the meaning of my life hasn't. That night on the bathroom floor I found that. My life is about being connected to other people. There's no goal, no lofty objective – it's just to be connected to other people. That's all."

I don't think Anastasia is all that different from most of us – although maybe her existential crisis was more dramatic than most. Many of us have to answer similar questions for ourselves. Why am I here? Why do I suffer? Can I stand the suffering? Is there any meaning in this strange experience of living? Why persevere? I've certainly had to ask myself those questions, especially when my life seemed a mess, off-track, or just confused.

Anastasia taught me that each woman has to find her own answers. I cannot simply adopt someone else's reason for living and make it my own. I think life asks us each to struggle with tough times, wrestle with our demons, and dig deep to find what we need to continue.

Someone wise once said, "Pain is the touchstone of spiritual growth." Anastasia has certainly lived that maxim, and so have I. It's hard, very hard sometimes. But I don't know of any alternative. As far as I can tell, the only way out is through.

Some rainy winter Sundays when there's a little boredom, you should always carry a gun. Not to shoot yourself, but to know exactly that you're always making a choice.

—Lina Wertmuller, Italian film director

Surviving means being born over and over.

—Erica Jong, author of *Fear of Flying*

Life's challenges are not supposed to paralyze you; they're supposed to help you discover who you are.

—Bernice Johnson Reagon, composer, singer

If a Problem Has No Solution, It's Not a Problem, Just a Fact

MY FRIEND DIANA BARNWELL'S mother must have been very wise. I never met her, but from the stories Diana tells me, I know she was a remarkable woman. One of Diana's favorite sayings from her mother is, "There are no answers. . . . Pursue them lovingly."

At first glance, it seems like one of those Buddhist koans – a riddle with no answer. But upon deeper reflection, there is wisdom in her comment. In certain life situations, there is no good solution, no clear answer. There are only trade-offs, stand-offs, or stalemates. In such situations, the best one can do is to proceed with great caution, sensitivity, and loving kindness. There often is no "happy ending," and we must live with tension, anxiety, and lack of resolution. Love is the only guiding principle.

Diana was lucky to have such a wise, insightful mother. I'm lucky to have Diana as my friend.

Mother Goose

For every evil under the sun
There is a remedy or there is none
If there be one, seek till you find it
If there be none, never mind it.

10

Heart and Soul
of the Matter

There is a collective force rising upon the earth today, an energy of reborn feminine. She is peeking around corners, taking over businesses, tucking in children, and making men go wild in every way. She knows us at our source. She is not, as we are not, lacking in virtue. She remembers our function on earth: that we should love one another. She has come to reclaim us. She has come to take us home.

—Marianne Williamson, author,
spiritual teacher

What are we? Are we physical creatures who have spiritual experiences; or are we spiritual beings who are having a physical experience? I don't know the answer to that question any more than I know how many angels can dance on the head of a pin. But what I do know is that spirituality is important. No, it's more than just important. Ninety-eight percent of all Americans report that they believe in God — which tells me that spirituality is a central fact of almost everyone's life.

That's not to say that religion is important to everyone. Religion is not the same as spirituality. As Mary Lou O'Gorman writes, "Religion is the structure of your being and believing. Ritual gives order to your beliefs. Spirit, or spirituality, is the heart of a person — the 'stuff' of a life."

Perhaps all we can say for sure is that our questions about the meaning of life, our search for spiritual answers, and our longing to belong to something greater than ourselves lead us each down our own path — and that perhaps all our paths lead to the same place.

Good Karma for New Beginnings

I AM SO FORTUNATE TO LIVE in a multi-ethnic city like Los Angeles because I have the opportunity to learn from women who come from different cultures. Recently, over a cup of tea, I had a conversation with my friend from El Salvador, Leonor Gonzalez, who makes my life so much easier because she cleans my house and helps keep me organized. We started talking about how we had spent the recent holidays.

"On New Year's Day, I went to the hospital to visit a little boy," she told me.

"A family member?" I asked.

"No," she replied, "someone I never met before.... Remember that little boy who was in the newspaper about a month ago – he was from El Salvador and his stomach was real big?"

"Oh yes," I recalled. "He had some kind of terrible liver disease, didn't he?"

"That's right," she affirmed. "They couldn't find a donor, so his mother gave him part of her liver. A foundation made it possible for them to come here and have the surgery – otherwise he would have died in El Salvador.

"On New Year's Day, I tell my husband Victor that I want to go visit this boy in the hospital. We are from the same country and I thought it would be nice to go see him. Victor told me he didn't want to go. 'They'll never let you in,' he said, 'because you're not family.' I told him, 'I don't care. Maybe they don't let me in, but I'm going to try anyway.'

"I knew he was at Children's Hospital, so I went there with my sister and we asked the people at the front desk if we could visit the little boy from El Salvador. They called the nurses, who said, 'Sure, why not?' So we went upstairs to see him. I told him I saw him on television and that made him so happy. He was smiling and glad that we came to see him. I gave him an envelope with some money, because I know his family is very poor. This little kid, he is only eight, he looks at me and says softly, 'Do you want a receipt?' 'No,' I tell him, 'the money is for you, and I don't need a receipt.'"

"What a great thing to do!" I told Leonor. "Why did you do it on New Year's Day?"

"Because it's the first day of the year," she replied. "I want to start off my year doing something good for somebody. It makes me feel good. Who knows? Maybe it will come back to me, too, and it will be a good year. That's what I believe, at least." She smiled happily.

What startled me most about Leonor's story was how it echoed the advice I had received just a few weeks earlier from my Vietnamese manicurist, Lan Nguyen.

Lan and her three sisters-in-law work together in the nail salon, and it is fun for me to vicariously enjoy their big, extended family. We often talk about our children, our families, what new book I am writing, and whatever else is interesting in our lives. This visit, Lan asked me what my plans were for New Year's.

"I'm going to a friend's house for a party tomorrow night," I said, "then on New Year's Day I'm going to start work on my taxes.

The house is nice and quiet, and the phone doesn't ring, so it will be a good time to concentrate and get a head start."

She looked up from my hands, her eyes as big as saucers. "You shouldn't do your taxes on New Year's Day!" she exclaimed. "Bad luck!"

"What?" I asked. "Why?"

"Because," she answered, "whatever you do on the first day of the year sets the tone for whole rest of year! Taxes mean money goes out. You should do something that means money comes in! Do something else . . . no taxes!"

"Really?" I asked her.

"Yes!" she replied emphatically. "I tell you something – when I was a girl, on the first day of the year, I would get out my school books and spend some time doing studying. My family ask me why I was studying, since school was not in session, and I tell them, 'Because I want to have good year in school, and if I study today, it sets the tone for my whole school year. This way I will do well.'"

Lan was so earnest, I couldn't help but be convinced by her sincerity and experience. I smiled. "You know, Lan, that makes very good sense to me. I am going to take your advice. I won't do the taxes on New Year's. I'll plan a seminar I have to teach later in the month, or I will work on my book project – both of those things will bring in money. That will be good, right?"

"Right," she nodded happily, as she went back to work on my nails. "It will be a good year!"

Well, my year isn't over yet, but so far, so good.

Deep down in my soul
I hear the grandmothers whispering

—Harvest McCampbell, poet and herbalist

Perhaps they are not stars in the sky, but rather
openings where our loved ones shine down to let
us know they are happy.

—Eskimo legend

Giving Back to the Universe

A COUPLE OF YEARS AGO I was having a hard time financially. It had been a slow year for business; I'd had some big medical bills; and I had not been as careful with my money as I should have been. It was November, and I didn't know how I was going to make it through the end of the year. I called my friend Anna to ask her advice, because she has a good head for money.

I tearfully explained my predicament. She listened quietly. She was kind and sympathetic, completely understanding. She did not judge or scold. "You want my advice?" she asked, when I had finished.

"Well, sure," I replied, "that's why I called you."

"Tithe," she said simply.

I couldn't believe my ears. "You don't understand," I objected. "I just told you – I don't have any money coming in, I've got all these bills piled up, and I don't know how I'm going to meet the mortgage next month. I can't tithe – I have nothing to tithe with!"

"Well, you asked my advice, and I'm giving it to you," she said matter-of-factly. "All I have to share with you is my own experience. If you start to tithe, you shift your relationship with God. It is an act of faith in which you essentially say, 'I know I will be taken care of, so I can give this money back to God.' It works for me and it works for lots of other people I know, too."

I knew in my heart of hearts that Anna was right. Tithing was something I had wanted to do for a long time, but I was afraid –

afraid I would not have enough money to meet my needs, afraid to give away 10 percent of my income, and afraid of financial insecurity. I had heard other people talk about tithing in the past and, being a spiritual person, I liked the idea – but my fear always got the better of me.

"Here's what I'd suggest," Anna continued. "Why don't you call Naomi and ask her what her experience has been with tithing? Then decide if it's right for you."

I thanked Anna for her advice, and immediately dialed Naomi's number. She was more than happy to tell me about her experience with tithing. She had been in similar financial straits a few years earlier, and had reluctantly agreed to follow Anna's advice. She started by tithing to a twelve-step community of which she was a member, because Anna had instructed her to "give to the spiritual community that nurtures you." Naomi took a check to the office of this twelve-step program every time she got paid (she was self-employed in the real estate business). "The first time I tithed," Naomi told me, "I sold a $400,000 house the very next week! I made a great commission. I'm sure it was a direct result of my tithing."

After a while, Anna suggested that Naomi start tithing to her local synagogue, since she had been born and raised Jewish. "I'm not going to do that," Naomi protested. "I lost my faith years ago, and I'm not going to give them any money." Anna nudged Naomi, "Just try it. Do it a few times. See what happens." The next time Naomi got paid, she drove to the synagogue and gave them a check. Before long, the rabbi invited her to come to a special event at the synagogue. She went, met a few people she liked, and started going to more events. Her heart began softening toward the Jewish faith she had rejected, and over time she gradually became a part of this community and an official member of the temple.

About this time, her young nephew turned thirteen, old enough for his bar mitzvah. Knowing her sister didn't have much money, Naomi offered to pay for the bar mitzvah. Naomi had been estranged from her sister, but she loved her nephew very much. Over the months of planning the ceremony and the party, Naomi and her sister gradually worked through their differences and were reconciled. The bar mitzvah was a wonderful day for the whole family.

Naomi's commitment to tithe 10 percent of whatever she earned transformed her life. Tithing did more than put her on sound financial ground, it brought her back to her Jewish faith, strengthened the bond between her and her nephew, and reunited her with her sister. She was living a life of miracles.

The doubts I had about tithing disappeared upon hearing Naomi's story. Tithing means saying to God, "I trust that You will provide for me, and I am willing to give back 10 percent to do Your work in the world." Tithing lifts the burden of fear from my heart, and replaces it with trust. Tithing to a spiritual organization that gives me spiritual sustenance is the best way of saying "Thanks" for all that I have received.

I once heard Jack Canfield (co-author of *Chicken Soup for the Soul*) talk about tithing and its role in his life. He said, "Both my co-author and I have been tithing for many years, and we think it's an important part of our business success. (Their *Chicken Soup* books have sold over 60 millions copies.) But I have to tell you, it was a lot easier to write those checks in the early years, when they were smaller. It's kind of hard to sit down today and write tithing checks for $100,000!" I laughed when he said that. The truth is, that's a problem I'd love to have!

I've been tithing for two years now, ever since the phone conversations I had with Anna and Naomi. I don't sell real estate, and I haven't had the success of *Chicken Soup*, but my finances have stabilized and the peace of mind I feel is wonderful. Tithing shifted my relationship to God from one of "fearful child asking God's protection" to "adult partner with God" in doing good in the world. It feels wonderful.

I try to give to the poor people for love what the rich could get for money. No, I wouldn't touch a leper for a thousand pounds; yet I willingly cure him for the love of God.

—Mother Teresa, Catholic nun, humanitarian

Every day I live I am more convinced that the waste of life lies in the love we have not given, the powers we have not used, the selfish prudence that will risk nothing and which, shirking pain, misses happiness as well.

—Mary Cholmondeley, novelist

Lookin' for Love in All the Right Places

MY FRIEND BARBARA HAS SPENT a number of years actively involved in twelve-step programs. She has a compulsive-addictive personality and likes to describe herself as a life-aholic. "It's not alcohol or food or drugs that's the problem," she tells me, "The problem is that I don't know how to deal with life – that's why I call myself a life-aholic. Somehow I didn't learn some of those basic life skills as a kid, and I turned to mood-altering substances and activities to help me deal with the day-to-day stresses of life. I tend to feel like my nerves are on the outside of my skin, not the inside. I always want a little something to help take the edge off – a little ice cream, a glass of wine, a new blouse – anything to help make me feel a little better when life gets to be too much."

Her story about discovering her addictive personality is a story that many women can identify with. It's a story of looking for love in all the wrong places. Millions of women reach for something outside themselves in an attempt to feel better. Some of us reach for chocolate, others reach for a bottle, some reach for a credit card and head off on a shopping binge. Some women seek reassurance in addictive relationships with the wrong men, others become workaholics to calm their self-doubt with over-achievement. Some women resort to compulsive dieting and exercise to keep their demons at bay, others troop off to physicians to get prescriptions for the latest drug *du jour.* All of these women are essentially on the same quest.

They – no, we – are looking for a little something to make us feel better about ourselves and about life.

My friend Barbara is among the growing number of women who have given up looking for love in all the wrong places. She explains: "All along what I really wanted was a friend, a hug, a smile, someone to talk to, someone who really understood me, someone to love me. I didn't know how to get those things, so I reached for things I did know how to get – food, alcohol, prescription pills, and new clothes. They were legal and easy to get, and they seemed to work. The problem is, they didn't work long enough. I'd have to get another 'fix.' Over time, the things that used to make me feel better started to make me feel worse. Food was my best friend, but then it turned on me. I gained weight and hated myself. But I couldn't stop. My compulsive behavior was out of control – I was possessed by a demon I didn't understand.

"Once I found my way to twelve-step programs like Overeaters Anonymous and Debtors Anonymous, I found a solution. I found people who understood me and didn't judge me. I found a Higher Power, something larger than myself, in which I could put my faith and trust. I found the hugs, smiles, listening ears, compassionate hearts, and the unconditional love that I had wanted all along."

I think of Barbara when I find myself tempted to resort to sugar or shopping to make myself feel better. Sometimes I feel empty or anxious. I am torn . . . as she says, "torn between Godiva or God." Sometimes I still choose Godiva, but other times I remember to pick up the phone and call a friend, go for a walk, read a spiritual book, or simply bow my head and pray. Barbara, and other women like her, are teaching me how to look for love in all the right places.

> *Often people attempt to live their lives backward; they try to have more things, or more money, in order to do more of what they want, so they will be happier.*
> —Margaret Young

> *I'm fulfilled in what I do. . . . I never thought that a lot of money or fine clothes — the finer things in life — would make you happy. My concept of happiness is to be filled in a spiritual sense.*
> —Coretta Scott King, civil rights activist

What Does SERENITY Mean to Me?

Selflessness

Ego-reduction

Real peace of mind

Energy for life

No drama

Interest in others

Tranquility

"Yes" to God's Grace and Love

In Search of the Holy Gail

I WAS KEEPING NINA COMPANY one cool fall evening while she sipped soup in front of the crackling fire in the fireplace. She had come home from the hospital that morning, after an emergency appendectomy a couple of days earlier.

"Where's Sara?" I asked. Sara was Nina's roommate.

"She's at church tonight, Nina replied. "She's going through a covenant class, getting ready to join the church. She'll be home soon."

"I thought you two belonged to that evangelical church in Pasadena — are you switching churches?" I queried.

"Not me, just Sara," Nina said.

It wasn't long before Sara came home and joined us in the family room. Her eyes were bright, her face was glowing, she was bubbling with energy. She had brought another friend, Janis, home with her to visit with Nina for a while. "What a great session we had tonight!" Sara enthused. "BJ, you should come to this church with me sometime — it's great!"

"Naaaah," I shook my head. "I've tried that church a few times. It's not for me. It's a very pretty building, but I don't like the pastor's style. He's got 'the little man complex' — he's full of himself."

"Oh, that guy retired last year," Sara reassured me. "They've got a new guy now, and he's wonderful! You should come visit again — it's your kind of place."

"I wonder just what is my kind of place?" I asked out loud. "I've been looking for a spiritual home for such a long time, and I still haven't found it."

"What are you looking for?" Janis chimed in.

"Well, it's hard to articulate. I've tried conservative evangelical churches, liberal activist churches, nondenominational churches, New Age-y kinds of places, and finally I gave up on churches after a while. I want a place that doesn't have such a male, patriarchal theology – a place where women are fully equal to men, where the face of God is feminine as well as masculine. I don't know how to describe what I'm looking for. All I know is I've been on some life-long quest . . . like the search for the Holy Grail."

"Maybe in your case, it's the Holy *Gail*!" Sara joked. "You're looking for more feminine expressions of spirituality."

"Oooooh, bad pun," I groaned.

"Don't make me laugh!" Nina pleaded as she clutched her abdomen. "It hurts when I laugh!" At which point we all started to laugh.

The four of us had a wonderful discussion that evening about all things spiritual. I had studied theology in graduate school, and I told my friends about how confusing it was to read the writings of those dead European white guys – Neibuhr, Bonhoffer, Tillich, Schliermacher, and all the others: "I would read one, then another, and find myself torn and conflicted – who was right? Who had a handle on God? Invariably I ended up in tears, frustrated and anxious. One day I finally decided, A pox on all their houses! I wasn't any closer to understanding God than when I had started my studies. I was more confused, and definitely more upset. I think trying to reduce God to systematic theology is an act of hubris!" I told my professors, "Who are these guys who think that their puny little human brains can even begin to comprehend the enormity and mystery of the Divine? I'm not reading any more of this stuff!"

The sympathetic nods of my friends' heads as they listened to my story told me that they, too, had experienced some frustration in their search for the transcendent, the holy.

Janis shared with us the story of her own spiritual searching – which led her to Eastern traditions. "I like what Buddha taught – the only thing we need to do is wake up, become fully present in each moment," she told us. "Buddha didn't have a creation story, because we can never really know where we came from," she said. "Nor did he teach about a heaven or hell, because we can never really know what happens to us after death. All that's really important is the here and now, and living a good life in each and every moment. Buddhism is about living life as it is, not longing for some pie-in-the-sky reward after I die. I got a lot of peace from my studies of Buddha's teachings, not to mention the wonderful benefits of meditation."

Sara's story was quite different from Janis'. "I've done a lot of searching myself," she told us. "I was born and raised Jewish, but I became a Christian about ten years ago, and I just finished my masters degree in divinity at the seminary in Claremont. Now I'm thinking about continuing with a Ph.D. and becoming an

Episcopal priest. I'm a lesbian, to boot, so I guess that makes me really unique!" she finished, laughing.

"I thought I was pretty eclectic," I told Sara, "but you have really been all over the spiritual map, haven't you? What an amazing spiritual journey!"

"What about you, Nina?" Janis asked our invalid friend. "What do you think about God? Where do you turn for spiritual answers?"

"Well, I tend to think in metaphors ... so for me, God is like electricity," Nina replied. "Invisible, but powerful – and absolutely essential to living my life. I think about how I live in my house: the electricity flows throughout the house, giving me access to light, to warmth, even to different appliances, the TV, the computer, etc. The electric current is silent and invisible, but it is always there when I need it. I don't think about it most of the time, but I certainly rely on the security of knowing it's there."

"That's a wonderfully visual metaphor!" I interrupted.

"It seems to fit," she replied. "Electricity is silent and invisible, but it's very real. So is God. I stay plugged into the spiritual current by meditating and praying. I don't need to go to church for that – I can plug into God anytime, anyplace I want. God supplies the energy, the life-force that runs my life. It's pretty simple."

It was a wonderful evening – four friends talking about something really important in their lives, their spirituality. We had each walked different paths and taken many detours. Sometimes we stumbled and fell – other times our strides were steady and purposeful. Sometimes we felt hopelessly lost on our journey of faith — other times we knew we were right on target.

What I learned from my friends that evening is that while our own personal definition of God is important to each of us as individuals, it is not what's important to us as friends. Our theology is not what brings us together — it's not the teachings of any particular priest, rabbi, minister, or guru that makes us spiritual sisters. Sharing our experiences with one another is what's really important to us as we continue to walk our spiritual paths. I suspect that all paths ultimately lead to the same place. Many roads — one destination.

All religious language is really metaphor. God language does not really tell us about God, but it does tell us a considerable amount about those who use it.

—Rita M. Gross, teacher and writer on Kabbalah
and Jewish mysticism

Female Religion

The largest U.S. religious group that has a very clear female aspect of God is Mormonism, which is the fourth- or fifth-largest denomination in the United States (depending on whom you ask). There is a very explicit belief in a Mother in Heaven – not simply an "aspect" of God, but an actual female counterpart to God.

We all come from the Goddess
And to her we shall return
Like a drop of rain
Flowing to the ocean.

—Traditional womyn's circle song

Then that little man in black there, he says women
can't have as much rights as men, 'cause Christ wasn't
a woman! Where did your Christ come from? From God
and a woman! Man had nothing to do with Him.

If the first woman God ever made was strong enough
to turn the world upside down all alone, these women
together ought to be able to turn it back , and get it
right side up again!

—Sojourner Truth, author of *Ain't I a Woman?*

Everybody's an artist. Everybody's God.

—Yoko Ono, multimedia artist

Dear BJ,

Probably my greatest teacher is a woman I've never met - the Great Mother, Mother Nature, Gaia. While She has shown me the beauty of wildlife, wildflowers, and the awesome power of a sunset, probably the most powerful lesson She has taught me is to come as I am and try. Try to bear witness to the cycle of life and death and rebirth. Try not to tear down, but to sow slowly, with patience and purpose. The more I notice of the hummingbirds in my backyard, the weeds that grow in places they have no reason to be, and a worm that I accidentally cut in half while tilling the soil that becomes two worms, I'm redeemed and more deeply connected. I am imperfect in learning the lessons She teaches me, but She has endless patience to show me again. It's all about intention and connection.

Gratefully,

Wendy Menjou

flower essence consultant

What Is WISDOM?

Wondrous

Insight

Seeing

Deeply

Offering

Miracles

The Transformative Power of Love

MY FRIEND KIKANZA is the minister of a small Unity church, and she has a sign in front of her church that says, "Those who deserve love least need it the most." What a hard message to live! It is easy to love people who are sweet, agreeable, and pleasant. But it's hard to love people who are egotistical, cranky, or difficult – the jerks in our lives.

Kikanza is right in line with all the world's great spiritual traditions, emphasizing the power of love to transform people and situations. I do believe in the transformative power of love. I've read about it, and even seen it a few times in my life.

"But," I wondered, "Does this principle of unconditional love have any place in the business world? If love could transform people and relationships in our personal lives . . . why couldn't it do so in our work lives, too?" I decided to experiment with Kikanza's bit of spiritual wisdom.

I had a particular candidate in mind – someone with whom I have done business for several years. Elliot is a bright, talented, creative man, who is also cynical, pessimistic, and paranoid. His first response to almost all new ideas and proposals is "No." He sees danger and conspiracy everywhere, and fears that his business competitors will very soon do him in. He has a battery of attorneys, and he's quick to sic them on people at the slightest provocation. In short, he can be a difficult man to deal with.

My relationship with him had never been close and chummy,

but it started out okay. Over the past few years, our relationship grew more distant and strained. I even received a couple of his attorney-drafted letters, rattling his saber at me over some competitive threat he perceived in my activities. I grew to resent and dislike him. He grumbled to others about me, and I groused to others about him. We were much like two estranged former lovers whose romance had disintegrated – we were both sure it was the other person's fault.

I told Jason, one of my professional colleagues, about Kikanza's notion of "loving people who deserve it the least" and my idea about using this principle with Elliot. Jason, who also has a difficult relationship with Elliot, told me I was nuts. He wished me well, but expressed great skepticism about my idea. This was going to be a grand experiment in the power of love. I made a commitment to love Elliot unconditionally. I had no idea if it would work, but things weren't very good between us anyway, so what did I have to lose?

Elliot was a deeply unhappy man – insecure, fearful, riddled with doubt and anxiety. I suspected that he had been deeply hurt or disappointed many times in the past, and that it was his emotional or psychic wounds that made him such a difficult person to work with. I made my "diagnosis" of Elliot's problem, and wrote him a "prescription" – a massive infusion of unconditional love. I committed myself to greet his every action with love and compassion; to listen with love; to speak with love; to do business with him with profound love. Not the romantic, sentimentalized kind of love – but rather, a love that comes from a conscious commitment to maintain unconditional positive regard for this human being.

I called and set up an appointment with Elliot. When we got together, I told him I was concerned that our professional relationship seemed strained and distant. I talked about how I would like our working relationship to be. We shared perspectives with one another, and I looked at things from his view. I began to understand why he had interpreted events and situations the way that he had. We talked; we listened. It felt good to clear the air.

When I walked into the meeting that day, we were on opposite sides of the table, both literally and figuratively. When I left, our chairs were still in the same place, but our perspectives had shifted, so we now seemed to be on the same side of the table.

I wasn't at all sure that Elliot had changed in any significant way, but it didn't matter. I had begun my experiment, and I was content to have held the meeting. I was still committed to loving him.

I reported back to Kikanza as well as to my friend Jason. I didn't have any earth-shaking news to report, but I felt good for having carried through on my commitment.

Riding the BART train in San Francisco a few days later, I found myself looking at the people on the train with me. Old people, young people, black faces, white faces, fat people, skinny people, animated people, people sound asleep. Suddenly I was flooded with an incredible feeling of love for these people. These were strangers whom I would probably never see again, people I knew nothing about – and yet I fell in love with all of them. This unexpected sense of love filled me with happiness, and I smiled to myself, marveling at this great feeling.

I realized something then . . . my commitment to love Elliot had not transformed Elliot at all – it had transformed me! Unconditional love did not transform the one on the receiving end – it transformed the one who was doing the loving. My experiment in the power of transformational love had been successful – just not in the way that I had expected.

But, experiments are like that – particularly experiments with human subjects. Kikanza was right about loving the unlovable, but she was right in a way that I had not anticipated.

A final note: About eight months after my experiment, I called Elliot about a business matter. We talked about a difficult situation we both were experiencing with another company, and he surprised me with the generosity of his position toward that company. When I remarked on this new attitude, he replied with something that surprised me even more. He said, "Remember when you and I had that meeting a few months ago? Well, you reminded me of some of the values that I used to hold . . . and I realized that many of them had fallen by the wayside over the years. I decided that those values are still important to me, and I decided to make them a part of how I do business."

It was a moment of joyful surprise for me. That sign in front of Kikanza's church was right: People who deserve love least do need it the most. What the sign didn't say was, "And when you love the unlovable, who knows what miracles are possible?"

In "world-changing," it is absolutely essential that I be what I want to see. It is elegantly simple and most profound — "being" is an active verb.

—Betty Reid Soskin, Unitarian Universalist, community activist

I have found the paradox that if I love until it hurts, then there is no hurt, but only more love.

—Mother Teresa, Catholic nun, humanitarian

The truth is that there is only one terminal dignity — love. And the story of a love is not important — what is important is that one is capable of love. It is perhaps the only glimpse we are permitted of eternity.

—Helen Hayes, actress

In Closing . . .

THE WOMEN WHO HAVE TAUGHT ME important things are angels sent into my life, each one's lesson timed perfectly for what I needed to know in that moment. Like the ancient sage said, "When the student is ready, the teacher appears." My job has been simply to recognize those teachers when they show up, to learn as well as I can, and to put into practice what I've learned. Oh, and one more thing . . . to pass along to others what I have learned.

Such is the intent of this book — to gather women's wisdom, inspiration, and some practical skills as well, and put them in a package that makes it easy to share. If the women's lessons here add to your life even a fraction of what they have added to mine, I will have accomplished my goal.

"I am a pencil in the hand of God," Mother Teresa once wrote. I love that. In writing this book, I am a laptop in the hands of God.

Thank You!

Dear friends,

Life is lived in relationships, and relationships live in conversations. Creativity also lives in conversations, and this little book is proof of that. It was born in a conversation with my dear editor, Leslie Berriman. It came alive the moment she said, "Oooh, I like that idea.... That would make a lovely book."

Thank you, Leslie for your enthusiasm, encouragement, and your gentle sense of fun. Your editorial guidance was steady and true throughout. I especially love it when I hear you say, "You're there!"

I want to extend an enormous "Thank You" to the wise, wonderful women who have shared their stories with me for this book: Anita Goldstein, Joan Hill, Arleen Gevanthor, Judith Segal, Leonor Gonzalez, Diana Barnwell, Lan Nguyen, Janelle Barlow, Patti Riley, Leslie Yerkes, Sherry May, Brenda McCord, Ruth Pawluk, Wendy Menjou , Robin Lehman, Judy Wilson, Virginia Quirk, Patty Walters, Cheri Toomey Uno, and Maria Arapakis.

And "Thank You" to the many women who sent me quotes, facts, anecdotes, and great sources of material: Dana Kyle, Irene Fertik, Karin Offield, Karen Maguire,

continued

Phyllis Barr, Barbara Powers, Julie Hill, Rose Kemps, Jessica Overwise, Amy Berger, Patricia Fripp, Hannah Logan, Estelle Carlson, Linda Eremita, Nurete Brenner, Lynne Twist, Pat Jackson, Betty Reid Soskin, and the fabulous women in the Brain Exchange.

A very special "Thank You" goes to Alison Armstrong, who changed my life with all she taught me about men. (The men in my life thank you, too!)

"Thank You" to the wild, wonderful women at Conari - Suzanne Albertson, Jenny Collins, Heather McArthur, Brenda Knight, Julie Kessler, Rosie Levy, Maxine Ressler, and Leah Russell (oh yes, you too, Will Glennon and Don McIlraith!). Thanks to Pam Suwinsky for great copyediting. And a big hug of thanks to my terrific publicists, Leslie Rossman and Emily Miles Terry. It takes a Bevy of Babes to make a book successful!

Finally, a loving "Thank You" to the very special women in my family: Mom, Karen, Auntie El, Cousin Marilyn, and Cousin Doris. You have taught me many loving lessons over the years - I am deeply grateful.

Thank you one and all!
With much, much love,
BJ

For More Women's Wisdom . . .

BOOKS

Breaking the Glass Ceiling by Ann Morrison, et al. (New York: Perseus, 1994).

A Complaint Is a Gift by Janelle Barlow and Claus Møller (San Francisco: Berrett-Koehler, 1996).

Do As I Say, Not As I Did by Wendy Reid Crisp (New York: Berkley Publishing Group, 1997).

The Drama of the Gifted Child by Alice Miller (New York: Basic Books, 1996).

Just Like a Woman by Dianne Hales (New York: Bantam Paperback, 2000).

Living in the Light by Shakti Gawain (Novato, CA: New World Library, 1998).

Thinking in the Future Tense by Jennifer James (New York: Simon & Schuster, 1996).

Witty Words from Wise Women by BJ Gallagher (Kansas City: Andrews McMeel, 2000).

Women Who Shop Too Much by Carolyn Wesson (New York: St. Martin's Press, 1990).

other resources

"Celebrating Men, Satisfying Women" seminars

PAX Programs Incorporated

P. O. Box 693

Duarte, CA 91009

Phone: (626) 932-1904

Web site: www.understandmen.com

"Confidence, Composure, and Competence" and other audio programs

Maria Arapakis

SoftPower Resources, Inc.

435 St. Paul Street

Denver, CO 80206

Phone : (303) 331-0011

Fax: (303) 331-0066

E-mail: arapakis@quest.net

For seminars on "Everything I Need to Know I Learned from Other Women" contact:

BJ Gallagher

Peacock Productions

701 Danforth Drive

Los Angeles, CA 90065

Phone: (323) 227-6205

E-mail: bbjjgallagher@aol.com

Web site: www.womenneed2know.com

About BJ

BJ GALLAGHER is a storyteller, both by inclination and by profession. Her Irish heritage blessed her with a natural gift of gab, and her stories enrich and enliven the presentations she makes to groups of all sizes. "People forget facts and figures," she says, "but they remember good stories." BJ uses stories to teach important lessons about how to live a good life, create authentic relationships, nurture happy families, and do fulfilling work in the world.

Her own life story is as eclectic as the collection in this book. The daughter of a military family, she was "drafted at birth." She has lived in four countries on three continents, and in six states within the United States, from the littlest (Delaware) to the biggest (Texas). Although a native Californian, she is at home anywhere in the world. Her working life has run the gamut from cocktail waitress to corporate middle manager, including stints as intern in a congressman's office, secretary for a studio of graphic artists, sales trainer for car dealerships, ghost writer for a corporate CEO, career counselor, and university adjunct professor. She has been a stay-at-home wife as well as a single working mother with a latchkey kid. She is a Phi Beta Kappa graduate of the University of Southern California, and has earned her advanced degree from the School of Hard Knocks. Her crazy-quilt life has provided her with ample opportunity to hear and learn from other people's stories.

BJ has written eight books, including the international bestseller, *A Peacock in the Land of Penguins* (now published in thirteen languages worldwide). She gives keynote speeches for women's groups, as well as for corporate clients and professional associations. Her company, Peacock Productions, provides training programs as well as books, videos, and other learning materials and services to human resource professionals. BJ's other recent books are *Witty Words from Wise Women* and *What Would Buddha Do at Work?*

For more information, or to contact BJ for speaking engagements, please visit her Web sites: www.bjgallagher.com or www.peacockproductions.com.

To Our Readers

CONARI PRESS publishes books on topics ranging from spirituality, personal growth, and relationships to women's issues, parenting, and social issues. Our mission is to publish quality books that will make a difference in people's lives — how we feel about ourselves and how we relate to one another. We value integrity, compassion, and receptivity, both in the books we publish and in the way we do business.

As a member of the community, we donate our damaged books to nonprofit organizations, dedicate a portion of our proceeds from certain books to charitable causes, and continually look for new ways to use natural resources as wisely as possible.

Our readers are our most important resource, and we value your input, suggestions, and ideas about what you would like to see published. Please feel free to contact us, to request our latest book catalog, or to be added to our mailing list.

Conari Press
An imprint of Red Wheel/Weiser, LLC
P.O. Box 612
York Beach, ME 03910-0612
800-423-7087
www.conari.com